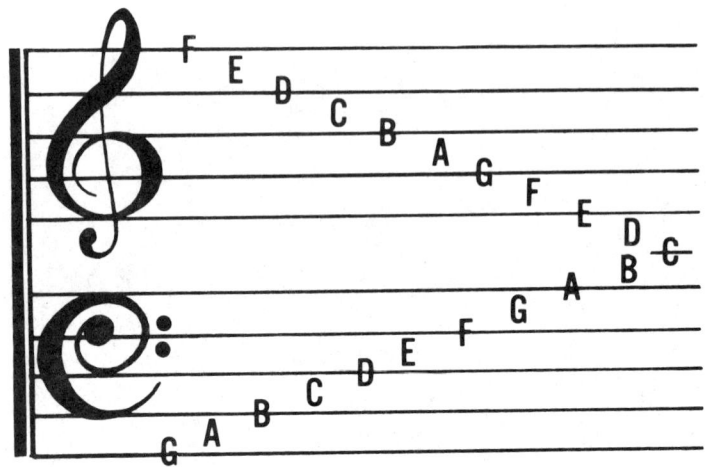

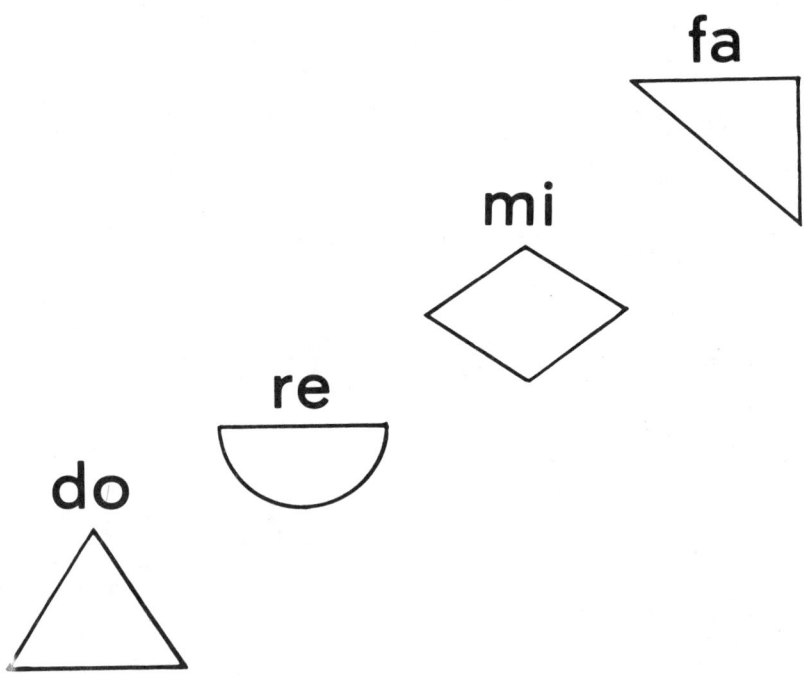

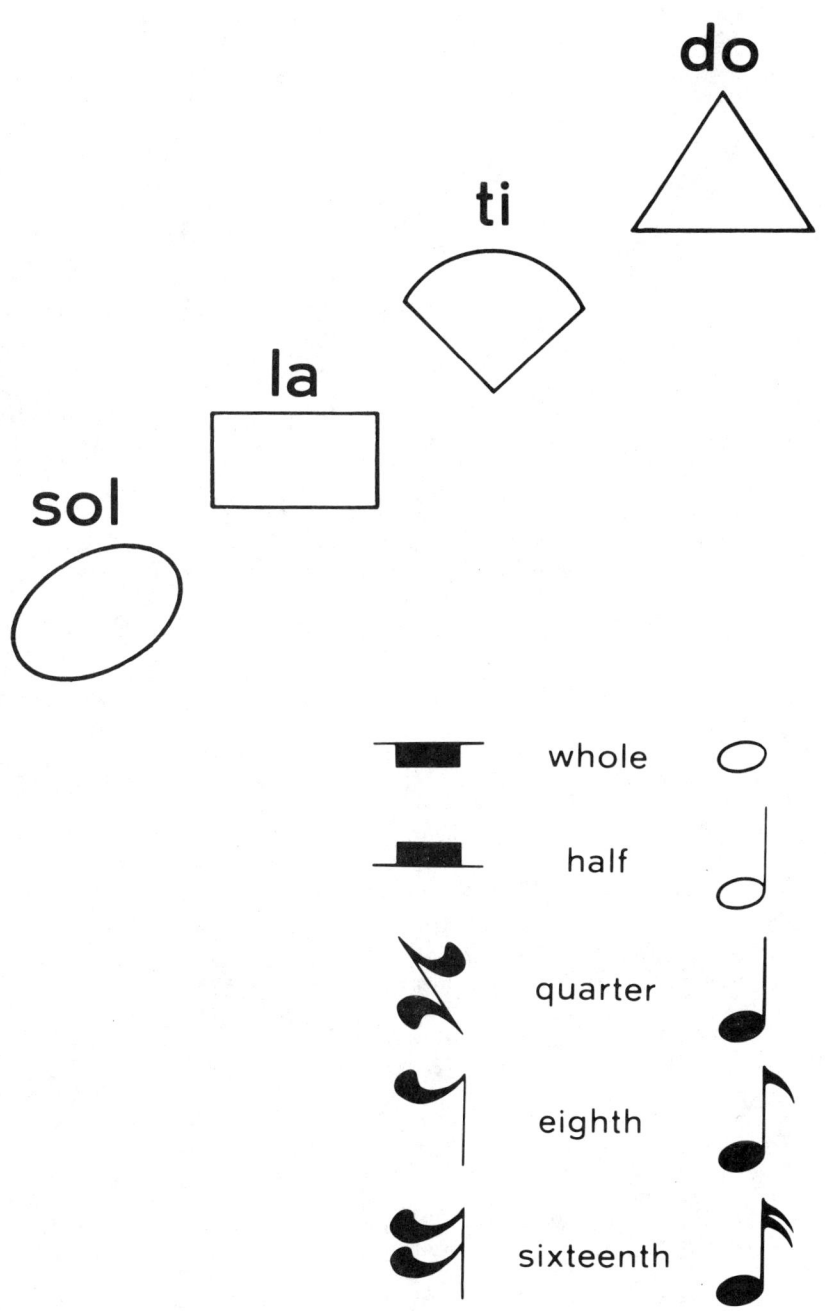

Christian Music Series

Book Two

Teacher's Manual

Series Titles

Developing in Music
Book Two
Teacher's Manual

Sing them o-ver a - gain to me,

Christian Music Series

Rod and Staff Publishers, Inc.
Crockett, Kentucky 41413

Telephone (606)522-4348

Acknowledgments

God has commanded us to sing, and singing is a part of the voluntary praise that we raise to our Maker.

The Bible tells us to sing with joy in our hearts, and that we should sing with the spirit and with understanding. This is the most important consideration in music. However, singing correctly is also an important part of worship. The purpose of this book and its subsidiary parts is to assist in the accomplishment of this objective.

We are grateful to the many individuals that have contributed to make this book possible. The writer is Joseph B. Keener. Harold Siegrist was the editor. The reviewers were Eby Burkholder, Boyd Campbell, and Paul M. Landis.

The teacher's manual, workbook, and test booklet were written by Marvin Eicher, and edited by Robert McDowell. The reviewers were the same as for the students' book.

Many other individuals have contributed in various ways to help bring this book and its parts to a completed form. We are indeed grateful for their faithful labors.

We are grateful to those who have granted permission for the use of copyrighted and uncopyrighted songs. If any permissions were overlooked, it will be adjusted upon receipt of proper information.

—The Publishers

Copyright, 1984

By

Rod and Staff Publishers, Inc.
Crockett, Kentucky 41413

Printed in U.S.A.

ISBN 0-7399-0600-3

Catalog no. 18691

7   8   9   10   11   —   18   17   16   15   14   13   12   11   10   09

Table of Contents

How to Use the Teacher's Manual

The purpose of this teacher's manual is to give clear direction to the music teacher, along with plenty of material with which to teach. The lesson titles in the teacher's manual correspond with the subtitles in the pupil's book, and there are separate instructions for teaching the lesson and for directing the singing. This plan allows you to have one lesson on music theory and one on singing, each week; or, depending on your schedule, you may have one longer music class each week and divide it in two periods.

"Teaching the Lesson" explains how to present the lesson concepts and conduct a class discussion centered around them. You may wish to have the students read each lesson themselves before you discuss it in class, or you could read the lesson together in class and then have the discussion. "Teaching the Lesson" is designed to give you additional matter to bring into the class discussion, and it should also prove helpful if you need further explanation of the lesson concepts for your own benefit. At the end of this section are instructions on what written work to assign.

Observe that the teacher's guide divides the pupil's text into twenty-three lessons and seven reviews for a total of thirty class periods. But you do not need to feel bound to this arrangement. Use more than one class period, if necessary, to assure that the pupils master the concepts in each lesson. This is especially important in chapters 3, 4, and 5, where many lessons build upon concepts taught in previous lessons.

"Conducting the Singing Period" suggests songs which can be used to illustrate what the lesson teaches. You will want to sing other songs, too; but these suggestions are given to help lend purpose to the singing period so that it does not become a mere twenty minutes of singing random selections. Have the pupils take an active part in telling how the songs relate to the lesson. The numbers in parentheses after the titles are the numbers of the songs in the *Christian Hymnal*; other titles refer to songs in the back of the pupil's book.

Standing for the singing period allows better breathing and gives the pupils a stronger feeling of participation. Also, if any of the suggested songs are new, try to learn some of them and then teach them to the pupils. Learning new songs regularly is an excellent way to maintain the pupil's interest in singing and to give them confidence in their ability to read music.

There is also a third part entitled "Quiz Questions," and it can be used in various ways. You may ask the questions during the class discussion, immediately afterwards, or at the next music class, sometimes as a "pop quiz." These questions are generally of a simpler and more objective nature than are the chapter and workbook questions.

The "Drill" section included in the teacher's manual for Book One, *Growing in Music,* of this series has not been incorporated in this book. There are occasional concepts that need special drill; and when that is the case, instruction for drill is given in "Teaching the Lesson." But you should certainly provide regular drill (with flash cards or some other means) if your students need it, especially if they have had little previous instruction in music. Be sure to tailor your teaching of music to what *you* see is necessary for *your* class.

Lesson 1

Music Is Important

Teaching the Lesson

Before you begin the teaching of the first lesson, have the pupils look through their books and observe the general outline and content. Show by the table of contents that the study of music is divided into various departments and that the chapters are built one upon another.

Now go into the main topic of lesson 1: music is important. The reason for the lesson is to teach that music is not an art which only a few gifted people can produce and enjoy. Rather, music is all around us; certain aspects of it such as rhythm are a basic part of our very make-up. While some children will readily agree with the main thrust of this lesson, others may be more reserved, especially if their past experience with music has been disappointing. The challenge for you is to teach music in such a way that it becomes important in the personal experience of each student.

You should point out that music is even more than pitch, melody, and rhythm. It is the listener's interpretation that finally determines whether a sound is music or noise. As "beauty is in the eye of the beholder," so music is in the ear of the listener. But as we study the composition of music and learn to appreciate its structure, we can enjoy as music that which did not really appeal to us earlier. Music written in the minor scale is one example.

Emphasize the encouragement and inspiration that can be received through singing. A look at several of the Scriptural accounts referred to in the lesson will be an aid in teaching this. Another account is found in 2 Chronicles 20, where we can read of a battle that was won through singing. And if you can relate an actual happening or personal experience in which music played a major part, you will make this lesson even more effective.

Assign exercise 1 in the workbook for written work.

Conducting the Singing Period

Emphasize hymns of praise and adoration. Suggestions:
"Holy, Holy, Holy" (12)
"What a Mighty God We Serve!" (16)
"Sing About Jesus" (5)
"The Comforter Has Come!" (132)

Quiz Questions

1. What are two things that produce music in the world about us? *(Birds, peepers, frogs, motors, etc.)*
2. Which is the most important kind of music? *(Singing by men, women, boys, and girls is the most important kind.)*
3. How are pendulums, hammers, saws, and rocking chairs related to music? *(They all have to do with rhythm, and music has rhythm.)*
4. What three kinds of music did Paul mention in his epistles to the Ephesians and the Colossians? *(Psalms, hymns, and spiritual songs.)*
5. When is singing more than entertainment? *(When it is used to redeem the time, to worship God, to encourage someone, or for some other worthwhile purpose.)*

Lesson 2

The Human Voice

Teaching the Lesson

This lesson is designed to provide a basic understanding of the marvelous "musical instrument" in the throat of every normal person. Mechanical instruments may stir the emotions, but they do not have either the richness of quality or the power of spiritual encouragement possessed by the human voice. Thus the human voice far surpasses mechanical instruments in its ability to produce music that is spiritually beneficial both to the listener and to the person who produces the music.

The vocal cords produce only the basic sound of the voice. The shape of the throat and the structure of the nasal passages are what add the quality by which we can recognize different people's voices. And for that marvelous phenomenon called speech, a complexity of tongue and lip movement that defies description must be performed to regulate the sound of the voice and produce comprehensible words. Add speech to the varying of pitch and volume required in vocal music, and you discover that singing is a marvel indeed!

Proper care of the voice includes the avoidance both of speaking or singing too loudly and of singing too high or too low. Boys especially should not strain their voices by trying to sing too low before their voices have changed. And no one should try to force his voice to perform normally when he has laryngitis, for that can do permanent damage to the vocal cords.

Assign exercise 2 in the workbook for written work.

Conducting the Singing Period

Sing hymns that contain references to the use of the voice in praising God, and point out the phrases that make those references. Suggestions:

15

"Oh, Could I Speak the Matchless Worth" (7) (Note stanzas 1-3.)
"Take My Life, and Let It Be" (397) (Note stanza 2.)
"There Is a Fountain" (118) (Note stanza 4.)
"Now Just a Word for Jesus" (197)

Quiz Questions

1. What is another name for the larynx? *(Voice box.)*
2. True or false: The larynx is composed of bones and muscles. *(False.)*
3. Describe the vocal cords. *(They are flat bands that vibrate when they are tightened and air passes through them.)*
4. How might a person harm his voice? *(By shouting or singing too loudly, especially when he has a cold.)*
5. What should be done when the voice becomes hoarse? *(The muscles surrounding the vocal cords should be relaxed.)*

Lesson 3

System of Study

Teaching the Lesson

As is true of other subjects, music can be subdivided into various components for an orderly system of study. Rhythmics, melodics, and dynamics may be considered the three dimensions of music: rhythmics pertains to its length, melodics to its height, and dynamics to its width. Chapters 2 through 4 of *Developing in Music,* Book Two, teach melodics, chapter 5 deals with rhythmics, and chapter 6 treats dynamics.

Review and drill the four properties of a tone, and associate them with the three departments of music introduced in the lesson. These are listed and classified here for your convenience.

rhythmics—length of tones—how long they are

melodics—pitch of tones—how high or low they are

dynamics—power and quality of tones—how loud or soft they are and what kind they are

Be sure your pupils understand the terms used in the lesson in connection with each department, so that they gain a proper concept of what each department includes. You can help them by discussing each term briefly, using the glossary. Then show why each term belongs in the department to which it is assigned. Clefs relate to melodics, for example, because the kind of clef indicates the letters that should be assigned to the degrees of a staff; and each letter refers to a tone of a certain pitch.

Counteract the tendency to neglect dynamics by pointing out its importance in relation to the words of a song. Show with examples that certain songs should be sung softly and rather slowly, whereas others should be sung faster and more spiritedly, because of their message and mood. If we stress melodics and rhythmics at the expense of dynamics, we emphasize the letter and ignore the spirit of the song.

To give dynamics its proper place in your class, ask the students regularly about the speed (tempo) and volume (power) at which songs should be sung. Have them make suggestions by referring to the words. Also remind them frequently about good singing habits: singers should sit or stand erect; they should open their mouths wide and enunciate clearly; and they should sing with light, clear voices that come through the mouth and not the nose. These are things that you should be observing every time your pupils sing together.

Assign exercise 3 and the questions at the end of chapter 1 for written work. Tell the pupils to be ready for a test on chapter 1 by the next music class.

Conducting the Singing Period

Emphasize dynamics in this singing period, singing at an appropriate tempo and volume for hymns of varying moods and messages. Suggestions:
"Tread Softly"
"Holy God, We Praise Thy Name" (10)
"Open the Wells of Salvation" (371)
"Almost Persuaded"

Quiz Questions

1. Which department of music—
   a. deals with power and quality? *(Dynamics.)*
   b. has to do with pitch? *(Melodics.)*
   c. is the most likely to be neglected? *(Dynamics.)*
   d. deals with the length of tone? *(Rhythmics.)*
2. What are the four properties of a tone? *(Length, pitch, power, quality.)*
3. What unit of measure is used in referring to the length of a tone? *(The pulse.)*
4. The speed of vibrations determines pitch. What unit is used to measure this speed? *(Vibrations per second.)*
5. To which part of a song should we pay the most attention in order to do well in dynamics? *(The words.)*

Lesson 4

Review of Chapter One

Teaching the Lesson

The account of a hymn writer's life at the end of each chapter of the pupils' text is included to add human interest to the study of music. That is the primary purpose of the accounts; no exercises or test questions are based on them, although you will likely want to have some discussion of the accounts in class. Knowing something about a hymn writer enables a singer to put extra expression and feelings into the singing of his hymns. This is especially true when the singer knows the details behind the writing of a particular hymn.

Use the quiz questions to review the concepts taught in chapter 1. Then give the chapter 1 test.

Conducting the Singing Period

Review good purposes for singing, and continue to emphasize the dynamics of music. Suggested hymns:

"Glory to God on High" (15)

"The City of Light" (370)

"The Eventide Falls Gently Now" (110)

"Cling to the Bible" (140)

Observe your students' singing habits for the purpose of obtaining grades on their singing.

Quiz Questions

After you read each question, call on pupils at random to give the answers orally.

1. Why do we say that music is a part of our world? *(We hear music*

every day in the songs of birds, the hum of motors, and the songs of people. There is rhythm in our actions, in mechanical devices such as pendulums, and in various things in nature such as the ocean waves.)

2. What is the most important kind of music? *(The singing of men, women, boys, and girls.)*

3. Singing should do more than entertain; what should it do? *(It should edify and encourage, praise the Lord, and redeem the time.)*

4. What is it that vibrates and produces the sound of our voices? *(The vocal cords.)*

5. When should we be especially careful not to overuse our voices? *(When we have a cold.)*

6. Name the three departments of music and tell which tone properties belong to each. *(Rhythmics—length; melodics—pitch; dynamics—power and quality.)*

7. What unit of measure is used—
   a. in rhythmics? *(The pulse.)*
   b. in melodics? *(Vibrations per second.)*

8. Why is dynamics such an important department? *(Dynamics is what determines how effectively the message of a song is presented.)*

Lesson 5

Introduction to the Staff, and Clef Signatures

Teaching the Lesson

For those students who have studied Book One, *Growing in Music*, of this series, this lesson is basically review. Each line or space is called a degree so that we do not need to say "line or space" each time. The lines of the G clef staff can be lettered according to the first letters of the sentence "*E*very *g*ood *b*oy *d*oes *f*ine"; and the letters of the spaces spell the word *face*. But it would also be good to review instant recognition of the letters with the use of flash cards.

The letters of the F clef staff, however, are not drilled in Book 1; you can use flash cards to teach and drill these as well. Sentences by which these letters are remembered are "*G*ood *b*oys *d*o *f*ine *a*lways" and "*A*ll *c*ows *e*at *g*rass."

Clef signatures should also be familiar to the students. Why C, F, and G are singled out as the degrees to which they refer is not clear. But the clefs are useful in that they give us *some* point at which to begin when we letter various staffs. The G clef (or treble clef) and the F clef (bass clef) are the two that are most commonly used. Recognition of the C clef is taught in Book 1, but its function is not explained. Observe that the C clef staff spans the gap between the lower and the upper staffs when the two are joined by a brace into a grand staff:

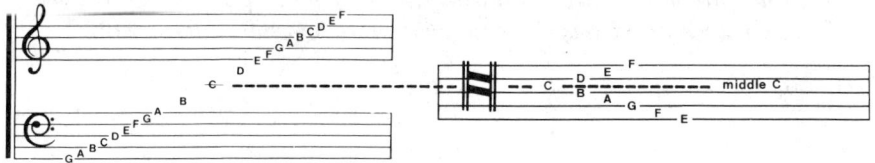

Assign exercise 4 as written work.

Conducting the Singing Period

Begin working with the singing of the parts (soprano, alto, and tenor), using the songs in the back of the pupil's book. The amount of teaching you will need to do depends on where your students are now. Alto and tenor are taught in *Growing in Music;* but if your students have not had much previous instruction, you will need to start from the beginning. In that case teach alto first, for the boys as well as the girls. Proceed to tenor only when the pupils have learned to sing alto well.

You should find these suggestions helpful when you teach a new part.

1. You sing the new part while the class sings soprano.
2. Have the whole class sing the new part together.
3. Sing the syllable names when learning a new part. First drill the shapes of the notes if necessary.
4. Have half of the pupils sing soprano and half sing the new part. Then switch sides.

Quiz Questions

1. What can we call each line or space of the staff? *(A degree.)*
2. How many degrees does a staff have? *(Nine.)*
3. Why are short lines sometimes added above or below the staff? What are they called? *(To create more degrees; ledger lines.)*
4. How many letters are in the musical alphabet? Name them. *(Seven: A, B, C, D, E, F, G.)*
5. The G clef makes which line G? The F clef makes which line F? *(The second line; the fourth line.)*
6. The C clef is used in what kind of music? *(In music for men's voices.)*
7. Two staffs joined by a brace are called what? *(A grand staff.)*
8. Where are the notes for the four singing parts found? *(Soprano and alto notes are found on the upper staff of the grand staff, and tenor and bass notes are found on the lower staff.)*

Lesson 6

Absolute Pitch, and the Functions of Accidentals

Teaching the Lesson

Absolute pitch, as the term indicates, means pitch as defined in mathematical terms. Each tone to which a letter is assigned has a fixed number of vibrations per second (vps) as indicated by this table.

C—261.6	G—392.0
D—293.7	A—440.0
E—329.6	B—493.9
F—349.2	C—523.3

As stated in the lesson text, the frequency of the first C given above is middle C—midway between the upper and lower staffs of the grand staff. The second C has exactly double the frequency of middle C, and it is an octave higher. Low C, on the bass clef staff, has a frequency of 130.8 vps and is an octave lower than middle C. Thus the frequencies may be doubled or halved to produce tones an octave higher or lower, but the new tones are still called by the original letters.

We use the term *absolute pitch* to emphasize that there is a definite, unchanging frequency of vibration to which each letter of the musical alphabet refers. The pitch of A always has 110, 220, 440, or 880 vps, according to the degree upon which it is placed. And in order to produce a tone of exactly the right pitch, we need a mechanical device such as a pitch pipe or a tuning fork.

After an absolute pitch is sounded, the other tones are determined by the system of relative pitches in the scale. Thus the scale may be considered a system of relative pitches based upon the absolute pitches of the staff. Chapters 3 and 4 teach this concept in detail.

A note placed upon any degree of any staff indicates the tone of that degree (called its natural tone). But the pitch may be altered by a sharp or a flat, which means that the note should be sung a half step higher or lower than its natural tone. A sharp or flat that is used as an accidental is never placed upon a degree which has a sharp or flat in the key signature. If the music writer wishes to alter the pitch of a note on such a degree, he uses a double sharp or a double flat. (Lesson 7 explains this in detail.)

Assign exercise 5 for written work.

Conducting the Singing Period

When you blow the pitch to start each hymn, tell the pupils its letter name to remind them of absolute pitch. Suggestions:

"Abide With Me, I Need Thee" (368)

"Yield Not to Temptation" (441)

"A Shelter in the Time of Storm" (515)

"Something to Do" (192)

Quiz Questions

1. What determines the pitch of a musical tone? *(The number of vibrations per second.)*
2. What do we call a pitch when it has a letter name and a certain number of vibrations per second? *(An absolute pitch.)*
3. What is the function of a sharp? A flat? A natural? *(To raise the pitch of a degree by a half step; to lower the pitch by a half step; to cancel the effect of a sharp or flat.)*
4. What is the name of the group of sharps or flats used at the beginning of the staff? *(A key signature.)*
5. What do we call a sharp or flat that is not in the key signature? *(An accidental.)*

Lesson 7

Naturals, Double Sharps, and Double Flats

Teaching the Lesson

This lesson concentrates on the effects of naturals, double sharps, and double flats. The natural is the simplest of the three in that it gives a note the natural pitch of the degree upon which it is placed, no matter what the pitch would be otherwise. The double sharp and the double flat, in essence, have the same effect as a single sharp or flat in relation to the other pitches in a melody. The only reason for their use is that the degree has already been sharped or flatted by the key signature.

A singer must observe whether the key signature consists of sharps or of flats if he is to sing a note correctly that has a natural before it. This is important because in vocal music we depend heavily upon a system of relative pitches—the scale. But those who play musical instruments simply sound the tone that is normally assigned to that degree of the staff. This is why the scale is more important in vocal music than in instrumental music.

It takes practice to be able to sing a note correctly if it has an accidental before it, because a person must learn to judge just how far above or below the usual tone he should go. That is, he must develop a feel for half steps. A good way to develop this skill is to concentrate on the distance between *Ti* and *Do*. Then, for a note with a flat before it, sing the note as it would be sung without the accidental but call it *Do* (no matter what it actually is). Now drop down to *Ti*, and you will have the correct pitch. If the accidental is a sharp, call the note *Ti* and step up to *Do*.

This method can be dropped once the sense is well developed. In fact, when a singer has a good feel for harmony, he can even sense where there *should* be a half step in the alto, tenor, or bass.

Assign exercise 6 for written work.

Conducting the Singing Period

Point out the accidentals in the suggested hymns. Are you singing them correctly? Suggestions:

"What a Friend We Have in Jesus" (350)

"Open the Wells of Salvation" (371)

"What a Mighty God We Serve!" (16)

"Weighed in the Balance" (294) (Observe the double sharp in the tenor of the last score.)

Quiz Questions

1. Explain how the natural received its name. *(The natural cancels the effect of a sharp or flat and returns a degree to its natural pitch.)*
2. Where is a double sharp or double flat used? *(On a degree that is sharped or flatted in the key signature.)*
3. A note with a double flat before it is sung only a half step lower than other notes on the same degree. Why? *(The degree is already lowered a half step by a flat in the key signature.)*

Lesson 8

Rules for the Use of Accidentals

Teaching the Lesson

This lesson deals with the rules governing the function of accidentals, and with the effect of accidentals on the size of intervals.

Rule 1 prevents the confusion that would result if an accidental affected all the degrees of a given letter name. In that case, a sharp on space C of the upper staff would also make middle C a half step higher, along with space C of the lower staff. Then a bass singer would also have to keep an eye on the G clef staff. But a sharp in the key signature causes no confusion, even though it affects all the degrees of the same letter name, because of the familiar series of steps and half steps in the scale. In fact, there would be quite a bit of confusion if the key signature did *not* affect all the degrees of the same letter names.

Rule 2 and Rule 3 are complementary. If the effect of an accidental ends at the next measure bar, then one would expect its effect to continue throughout the measure in which it is found. Observe also that an accidental affects only the notes found *after* it, not before it, on that degree.

The pupils who have studied Book One, *Growing in Music,* should remember the pattern of steps and half steps that occurs on the scale. Half steps occur between E and F, B and C, and a look at the table of frequencies in the teacher's guide for lesson 6 reveals that a half step is a much smaller change in frequency than a whole step. It should seem obvious that an accidental changes the size of the interval both above and below an original tone.

Assign exercise 7 and the questions at the end of chapter 2 for written work. The students should prepare for a test on chapter 2.

Conducting the Singing Period

Continue to stress the correct singing of accidentals. Point out how the rules in the lesson are followed where they apply in these suggested hymns:

"The Cross Is Not Greater" (427)

"Near to the Heart of God" (50)

"The Hand That Was Wounded for Me" (106)

"Love Divine, All Love Excelling" (43)

Quiz Questions

1. A sharp or flat sometimes affects all the degrees of the same letter name and sometimes only one degree. Explain. *(When a sharp or flat is in the key signature, it affects all the degrees of the same letter name. When it is used as an accidental, it affects only one degree.)*
2. What two musical symbols may cancel an accidental? *(A natural or a measure bar.)*
3. How many intervals are in the scale? How are they measured? *(Seven; in steps and half steps.)*
4. If there is a sharp on line G, what is the size of the interval between G and A? *(A half step.)*

Lesson 9

Review of Chapter Two

Teaching the Lesson

Review chapter 2 with the quiz questions; then give the chapter 2 test.

Conducting the Singing Period

Make some reference to ledger lines, absolute pitch, and the observance of accidentals during this period. Also remind the pupils about the importance of dynamics, and observe their singing for the purpose of obtaining singing grades. Suggested hymns:

"Bringing In the Sheaves" (187)

"Faith Is the Victory" (456) (Note the naturals in the third score.)

"Shine in My Heart, Lord Jesus" (385) (Observe the sharp in the soprano of the third score.)

"Jesus, Saviour, Pilot Me" (501)

Quiz Questions

Call on students at random to give the answers orally.

1. Give the musical term for each description:
   a. Short, added lines above or below the staff. *(Ledger lines.)*
   b. A word that means "line or space." *(Degree.)*
   c. A symbol that shows which letters should be placed on a staff. *(Clef signature.)*
   d. Two staffs joined by a brace. *(Grand staff.)*
   e. A sharp or flat not in the key signature. *(Accidental.)*
2. Which line is given an absolute pitch name by the G clef? By the F clef? *(The second line; the fourth line.)*

3. What are the four singing parts for which notes are placed on the grand staff? *(Soprano, alto, tenor, and bass.)*

4. How do we define an absolute pitch such as A? *(In terms of its number of vibrations per second.)*

5. Tell when each symbol should *not* be used as an accidental:

   a. A sharp. *(When the degree is flatted in the key signature.)*

   b. A natural. *(When the degree is not sharped or flatted.)*

   c. A double flat. *(When the key signature is made of sharps.)*

6. A sharp or flat changes the size of what? *(Intervals.)*

Lesson 10

Introducing the Scale,
Different Kinds of Scales,
and the Major Diatonic Scale

Teaching the Lesson

The word *scale* comes from the Italian word *scala*, which means "ladder." And that is a very fitting comparison; singing the scale gives a definite feeling of ascending or descending a ladder. It is true that some of the "rungs" are closer together than others, but for some reason the scale sounds best that way. You could use a pitch pipe to show how the scale would sound if it consisted of all whole steps. Begin at the lowest pitch and blow into alternate holes until you reach the highest pitch. For a C pitch pipe the progression would be: C, D, E, F$^\sharp$, G$^\sharp$, A$^\sharp$, C.

This demonstration shows two things: a whole-step scale sounds strange, and it has only seven tones. The tones of such a scale do not harmonize well either. So we find again that music is more than mechanics, for it also depends on what is pleasant to the ear.

The major diatonic scale is based upon the series of natural tones from middle C to high C. Since half steps occur between E and F, B and C, the pattern of the major diatonic scale agrees:

C	D	E	F	G	A	B	C
Do	Re	Mi	Fa	Sol	La	Ti	Do

This is why no sharps or flats are needed when the scale in the key of C is placed on the staff. But the details of staff and scale relationships are taught in chapter 4 rather than here. The staff shows absolute pitch, whereas the scale is a system of relative pitch that can be placed at various locations on the staff.

The names of the scale tones are called syllables because they are taken from the beginnings of longer words in a Latin hymn. In that hymn each line begins with a note that is one interval higher until the whole scale is covered. Here are the words: *Ut, Resonare, Mira, Famuli, Solve, Labii.* The two words of the last phrase are *Sancte Iohannes,* and they seem to have been combined to form the syllable *Si* which was later changed to *Ti.* The *Ut* of the first and last tones was eventually changed to *Do.*

Assign exercise 8 for written work.

Conducting the Singing Period

Begin using the sight-reading drills in the back of the pupil's book to practice the scale. You can use these as warm-up drills at the beginning of the singing periods, especially before the students learn a new song or singing part by reading the notes. Or if you prefer, you may use the sight-reading drills in connection with "Teaching the Lesson."

With this lesson, place the shaped notes on the board for some practice with the entire scale, and then sing selections from the first page of the sight-reading drills. Here are suggested hymns for use in the singing period:

"Joy to the World!" (92) (Observe that this hymn begins with the descending scale.)

"Come, Thou Almighty King" (1) (The first and the fourth notes of the second score are an octave apart.)

"O Happy Home, Where Thou Art Loved" (558)

Quiz Questions

1. In which department of music do scales belong? *(Melodics.)*
2. The scale is like a ———. *(ladder or stairway)*
3. Why do the tones of the scale blend well? *(Because they are orderly.)*
4. What is the difference between a degree and an interval? *(A degree is a line or space of the staff. An interval is the distance between two tones of the scale. Both degrees and intervals are measured in steps and half steps.)*
5. What kind of scale has both steps and half steps? What kind

has only half steps? *(A diatonic scale; the chromatic scale.)*

6. The beginning and ending tones of a scale are called its ——,
   and the syllable name of both tones is —— in the major scale.
   (home tones; do*)*

7. What do we call the distance from low *Do* to high *do? (An octave.)*

8. Where are the half steps in the major scale? *(Between* Mi, Fa
   and between Ti, Do.*)*

Lesson 11

The Minor Diatonic Scale

Teaching the Lesson

The minor scale is among the least understood and the least used of the systems in music. As suggested in the lesson, the probable reason for this is that a song written in the minor scale creates such strange feelings—feelings of sorrow and awe that are not often experienced otherwise. Lesson 12 expands on the moods of the diatonic scale and explains the feelings in more detail. Remember that music involves human perception; it is not the mere arranging of tones by fixed laws.

The intervals between the adjacent tones in the minor scale are exactly like those in the major scale: there are half steps between *Ti* and *Do, Mi* and *Fa,* and all the other intervals are whole steps. But there is an important difference in that the intervals between the first, third, and fifth tones are of different sizes. (These are the tones that determine the mood of a scale; see lesson 12.) In the major scale, the interval between *Do* and *Mi* is 2 steps, between *Mi* and *Sol* is $1\frac{1}{2}$ steps, and between *Sol* and *Do* is $2\frac{1}{2}$ steps. The minor scale has $1\frac{1}{2}$ steps between *La* and *Do,* 2 steps between *Do* and *Mi,* and $2\frac{1}{2}$ steps between *Mi* and *La.* The difference in the sizes and locations of these intervals, along with the feelings of the first, third, and fifth tones of the minor scale, is what creates the minor scale mood.

It is not always easy to recognize a song written in the minor scale just by looking at it. The major clues are that such a song usually begins with *La* or *Mi,* and (of course) that it has the peculiar mood of the minor scale. Be sure to sing at least one minor hymn so that your students can experience the feelings associated with the minor scale.

Assign exercise 9 in the workbook for written work.

Conducting the Singing Period

Have some practice with the minor scale. Sing the minor hymn "On Jordan's Stormy Banks I Stand," and then sing the same words in the major scale if possible. This will be a definite aid in showing the difference between the two kinds of scales.

Also sing other minor hymns that you know. Here are several suggestions from *The Church Hymnal.*

"Great God, How Infinite" (21)

"It Is Finished" (114)

"Stricken, Smitten, and Afflicted" (118)

"O Sacred Head Now Wounded" (121)

Quiz Questions

1. Why is the minor scale often discredited? *(Because of the strange feelings it creates.)*
2. In what two ways is the minor scale like the major scale? In what two ways is it different? (Any two in each group: *Likenesses— same syllable names, some whole and some half steps, half steps between* Mi *and* Fa, Ti *and* Do. *Differences—half steps located at different places, different home tones, different moods.)*

Lesson 12

Moods of the Diatonic Scale

Teaching the Lesson

Lesson 11 should have established the fact that the minor scale has a definite mood. In this lesson the pupils learn that the major scale also has a mood—something that often goes unobserved. Comparing the two as this lesson does will help to impress the concept of moods distinctly upon the students' minds.

A note of caution, however, is in order. Music does affect the emotions; and if it is used to cheer someone up who is discouraged through sickness or other adverse circumstances, it is indeed a benefit and a blessing. This was what singing did in the case of Paul and Silas in prison. But music can also create an artificial sense of well-being even when there is a serious spiritual need in the listener's life. The use of music to cheer King Saul is an example of this. So we must be sure that our despondency is not caused by spiritual needs before we resort to music to make ourselves feel better.

Observe that the feeling of each note in the scale is based upon its *relative* pitch. That is, when C is the key of the scale, the pitch of C is *Do* and that pitch is "firm and restful." But when the key is E, the pitch of C becomes the syllable *La* and it is "sad." A tone must be heard in relation to the other tones of the scale before it has a feeling.

Assign exercise 10 for written work.

Conducting the Singing Period

Practice both the major and the minor scales, and then use the second page of sight-reading drills for more practice. Again sing a minor hymn or two and call attention to the mood. Then sing some hymns of various moods in the major scale. Suggestions:

"Walking in the Sunshine" (440)
"Majestic Sweetness Sits Enthroned" (18)
"Work, for the Night Is Coming" (189)
"I Love to Steal Awhile Away"

Quiz Questions

1. What is meant by mood? *(Mood is a frame of mind or state of feeling.)*
2. Why can music influence a person's mood? *(Because music has feeling.)*
3. What is the general mood of the major scale? *(Being confident and at ease; being happy and contented.)*
4. What is the general mood of the minor scale? What are its three specific moods? *(Thoughtful and serious; sad, majestic, and terrible.)*
5. For each of the three specific moods of the minor scale, give one subject for a suitable hymn. *(Sad—the sufferings and death of Jesus. Majestic—the greatness and glory of God. Terrible—the judgments of God.)*

Lesson 13

The Chromatic Scale

Teaching the Lesson

In early music notation a note that was to be sung a half step lower or higher than normal was shown in color. This is why the scale of half steps is called the chromatic scale, although we now use sharps and flats instead of colors.

The ascending chromatic scale can be heard by starting at the lowest pitch of a pitch pipe and sounding all the tones in order to the highest tone. The descending scale can be heard by the reverse procedure. The many half steps are not very common in vocal music, although they occur regularly in instrumental music. Therefore, a person can learn to sing well without being able to sing the chromatic scale.

But as we saw in lesson 7, a singer does need to develop a feel for half steps if he is to sing correctly a note with an accidental before it. Drilling the chromatic scale is another excellent means by which to develop that feel. It will probably be difficult the first few times if you and the pupils are not accustomed to it, and you may need to stop and use your pitch pipe occasionally to make sure you are on course. But the singing of accidentals becomes very much simpler when one is well drilled in singing the chromatic scale.

Having put forth the effort to learn half steps, the students will probably be surprised when you tell them there are actually *two* tones between pitches that are a whole step apart. The pitch of A , technically, is just a bit lower than B , and the syllable *Ri* is slightly below *Ra*. These differences can be heard on certain musical instruments, and there are singers who can produce an A that is different from a B . But most musical instruments and most singers use a system of "equal temperament" and produce only one half step between each whole step.

Assign exercise 11 and the questions at the end of chapter 3 for written work. Tell the students to prepare for a test on chapters 1-3, concentrating most on chapter 3.

Conducting the Singing Period

Give some practice with the chromatic scale, and use the third of the sight-reading drills. Then sing some hymns that have flatted key tones, sounding also the tone that is a half step higher to show the small difference. With the first suggested hymn, for example, blow the key of E in addition to E♭. Suggestions:

"Tell Me the Story of Jesus" (317)

"God Will Take Care of You" (480) (Note the succession of half steps in the first score.)

"Send the Light" (212)

Quiz Questions

1. In what two ways is the chromatic scale different from a diatonic scale? *(The chromatic scale has thirteen tones whereas a diatonic scale has eight tones. All the intervals in the chromatic scale are half steps; in a diatonic scale most of the intervals are whole steps.)*

2. What are the added tones of the chromatic scale called? *(Chromatic tones.)*

3. Explain the difference between the ascending chromatic scale and the descending chromatic scale. *(In the ascending scale, the vowel in the syllables for the chromatic tones is* i *pronounced* ē. *In the descending scale it is* e *pronounced* ā.

4. What kind of accidentals are used with the ascending chromatic scale? With the descending scale? *(Sharps; flats.)*

Lesson 14

Review of Chapters One to Three

Teaching the Lesson

Use the quiz questions for review, then give the test on chapters 1-3.

Conducting the Singing Period

Sing selections from the first, second, third, and sixth sight-reading drills. Review the chromatic scale, both ascending and descending. Sing at least one minor hymn, as well as other hymns with varying moods. Suggestions:

"Awake, Awake, O Earth"

"Under His Wings" (525) (Observe the series of half steps at the beginning.)

"O Lord, Within My Soul" (333)

Since you are now halfway through the book, this would be a good time to check a number of things concerning your pupils' singing. Do they sit and stand erect and breathe correctly? Do they sing at a volume and tempo suitable to the words without being constantly reminded? How are they doing with part singing?

How many new songs have you and the pupils learned by reading the notes?

Quiz Questions

1. What two elements of music are found every day in the world about us? *(Pitch and rhythm.)*
2. What is a good purpose for singing? What is a wrong purpose? *(Good: to praise the Lord, to encourage someone, etc. Wrong: to show off one's singing ability, for mere entertainment.)*

3. Name the department of music in which each set belongs:
   a. Pitch, clef, harmony. *(Melodics.)*
   b. Volume, tempo, voice culture. *(Dynamics.)*
   c. Pulses, rests, measures. *(Rhythmics.)*
4. Which line is made G by the G clef? Which is made F by the F clef? *(The second line; the fourth line.)*
5. A C clef gives the degrees of the staff the same letter names as which other clef? *(The G clef.)*
6. What is the reason for the term *absolute pitch?* *(An absolute pitch does not change; it always has the same number of vibrations per second.)*
7. What is the function of an accidental? *(To raise or lower a note by a half step.)*
8. How long does an accidental have its effect? *(Throughout the measure in which it is found, unless there is another accidental on the same degree.)*
9. What is a scale? *(An orderly arrangement of tones.)*
10. Name and describe the three kinds of scales. *Major diatonic scale—eight tones, some whole steps and some half steps, home tone is* Do. *Minor diatonic scale—eight tones, some whole and some half steps, home tone is* La. *Chromatic scale—thirteen tones, all half steps, home tone is* Do.)
11. Besides the different home tone, what is the most important way in which the minor scale differs from the major scale? *(Its mood is different.)*
12. What vowel is used in the syllable names of the chromatic tones in the ascending scale? In the descending scale? *(The vowel is* i *pronounced* ē; e *pronounced* ā.

Lesson 15

What Is a Key, and What Is a Key Signature?

Teaching the Lesson

The first sentence in the pupil's text suggests that a key and a scale are very nearly the same thing. And that is a fact, for each is a family of tones. The difference is that a key is fixed whereas a scale is movable. If the beginning tone of the scale is fixed as an absolute pitch (A, B, C, and so forth), the result is a key. Thirteen different keys are possible because the beginning tone of the scale can be fixed at any one of the thirteen pitches of the chromatic scale.

But placing the scale on the staff is not as simple as it may appear from figures 30 and 31. The reason is the peculiar arrangement of steps and half steps in music, both on the staff and in the scale. The intervals match in the key of C, as we saw in lesson 10. In any other key there is at least one place where the intervals of the scale do not match the intervals of the staff. So it is necessary to place sharps or flats on certain degrees of the staff so that the intervals do agree.

As it works out, each key requires a different number of sharps or flats, and we can determine the key by counting the number of sharps or flats. The next two lessons on transposition teach exactly why each key requires the sharps or flats that are used to show it.

Assign exercise 12 for written work.

Conducting the Singing Period

Use the fourth page of sight-reading exercises for drill. Sing hymns with varying keys and point out the different locations of *Do*. Suggestions:

"Saviour, Teach Me Day by Day" (418)

"When I See the Blood" (307)

"Sweet Hour of Prayer" (353)
"How Firm a Foundation" (146)

Quiz Questions

1. How is the home tone and the scale related to the key tone and the key? *(When the home tone of the scale is fixed as an absolute pitch, the home tone is called a key tone and the scale is called a key.)*
2. What is used to make a key signature? *(Sharps or flats.)*
3. What do sharps and flats have to do with keys? *(They raise or lower certain degrees of the staff so that the intervals of the staff match the intervals in the desired key.)*

Lesson 16

What Is Transposition?
and Transposition by Fifths

Teaching the Lesson

With this lesson we enter a detailed study of what must be done when the scale is shifted (transposed) from one key to another. You can greatly simplify the complexities of transposition by the use of a visual aid such as the diagrams illustrated here. If the diagram of the scale is placed upon the diagram of the natural tones, it becomes obvious which degrees do not match and therefore need sharps or flats. It also becomes plain that in transposing by fifths, the half step between *Ti* and *Do* of the old key is the half step between *Mi* and *Fa* in the new key. By this method only one new sharp must be added for each new key signature.

The diagrams also show why sharps and not flats are used in transposing by fifths. In the key of G, for example, the syllable *Ti* is a half step higher than the natural tone F, and all the other syllables agree with the natural tones. So a sharp is placed on line F of both the upper and the lower staffs. Remember that a sharp or flat in the key signature affects all the degrees that have the same letter name. This is why no sharps are placed on the F spaces.

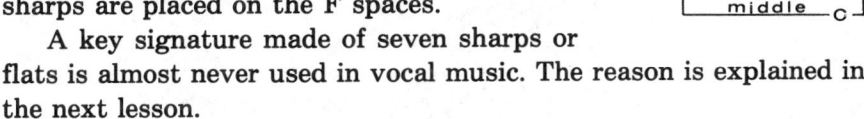

A key signature made of seven sharps or flats is almost never used in vocal music. The reason is explained in the next lesson.

45

Begin drilling instant key recognition by using flash cards with key signatures made of sharps. Assign exercise 13 for written work.

Conducting the Singing Period

Drill with scores A-E of the fifth sight-reading exercise, and review previous drills as you desire. The suggested hymns go through the order of transposition by fifths. Show that *Do* in each one is on the degree that was *Sol* in the previous hymn.

Suggestions:

"From Every Stormy Wind" (369) *Key of C*

"Somebody Follows You" (443) *Key of G*

"Walk in the Light" (450) *Key of D*

"I Would Love Thee" (452) *Key of A*

"In the Rifted Rock I'm Resting" (512) *Key of E*

"Rock of Ages, Cleft for Me" (521) *Key of B*

"Gone to Bloom Above" (626) *Key of F♯* (This is the only hymn in the *Christian Hymnal* in this key.)

Quiz Questions

1. What is transposition? transposition by fifths? *(Moving the key tone to another position on the staff; choosing the fifth pitch of one key for the key tone of another.)*
2. What must be done each time the key is transposed by fifths? *(A new sharp must be added to the key signature.)*
3. How do we recognize music that is written in the key of C? *(By the absence of sharps and flats.)*
4. The key of C is called the —— key. *(natural)*
5. What is the new key when the key of C is transposed by fifths? *(G.)*

Lesson 17

Transposition by Fourths

Teaching the Lesson

Transposing by fourths is in several ways the opposite of transposing by fifths. The most obvious way is that flats are used in the key signatures rather than sharps. Also, the half step between *Mi* and *Fa* of the old key becomes the half step between *Ti* and *Do* in the new key. The reverse is true in transposing by fifths.

Use your diagrams again as you discuss this lesson. Show that when *Fa* in the key of C becomes *Do* in the new key, the result is much the same as when the key of C is transposed to G. All the syllables match the letters of the staff except *Fa*, which is a half step too low. So a flat is placed on line B to make that degree of the staff match also.

But the flat on line B begins a series of transpositions in which *Do* is always flat instead of natural. Thus the key tones in all the subsequent keys are flat—B♭, E♭, A♭, D♭, and G♭. This series, in combination with the transpositions by fifths, allows all the half steps to be used as key tones for a total of thirteen keys (including natural C). all the key signatures for these can be written with six or fewer sharps or flats.

There are also key signatures of seven sharps or flats as shown in these two lessons. But they are rarely used because C♯ (for most purposes) is equal to D♭. Likewise, C♭ is equal to B. It is more logical to raise or lower five degrees by a half step than to change all seven of them—especially since the end result is the same.

This fact points to a general rule that is observed in writing key signatures: no more sharps or flats than necessary are used. It also shows how orderly music is: transpositions are very systematic; sharps and flats never need to be mixed in a key signature; and the key signature for a given pitch is usually written in only one way. Of the thirteen keys, the only ones that are identical in terms of absolute pitch are F♯ and G♭.

Add the key signatures made with flats to your flash card drill. Assign exercise 14 for written work.

Conducting the Singing Period

Sing scores F-I of the fifth sight-reading drill. The suggested hymns in this lesson go through the order of transposition by fourths, with *Fa* in one hymn becoming *Do* in the next. Suggestions:

"God Moves in a Mysterious Way" (85) *Key of C*
"God Is Love, His Mercy Brightens" (86) *Key of F*
"The Old Rugged Cross" (105) *Key of B♭*
"Lead Me to Calvary" (111) *Key of E♭*
"While the Days Are Going By" (182) *Key of A♭*
"The Lord of the Harvest Calls" (204) *Key of D♭*
"Be Ready When He Comes" (285) *Key of G♭*

Quiz Questions

1. The key tones in transposition by fourths are different from most of the key tones in transposition by fifths. How are they different? *(Most of the key tones are flatted instead of natural.)*
2. How is the key signature in transposition by fourths different from that in transposition by fifths? *(The key signature is made of flats instead of sharps.)*
3. When the key of C is transposed by fourths, is the new key F or F♭? Why? *(The new key is F; because F is not flatted in the previous key.)*
4. A key signature made of six flats actually indicates the same key as one made of six sharps. Why? *(The key of G♭ is the same as the key of F♯.)*

Lesson 18

Transposition and Key Signatures

Teaching the Lesson

The study of transposition may prompt this question: Why is transposition necessary? The answer is that some music has tones that are found chiefly at the upper end of the scale, some has more middle tones, some has lower tones, and some has the full scale. (See "Conducting the Singing Period.") Transposition allows us to sing a song in the range of tones that is best suited for that particular song. If the song is sung too high or too low, the voice will be strained unnecessarily and the effect will not be as pleasant as it should be.

It was already stated in lesson 17 that transpositions by fifths and by fouths are opposite in two ways. This lesson shows a third way: the order of the keys is exactly reversed. That may not be apparent from figure 53 until one realizes that the left half is to be read from right to left.

Observe that in figures 55-57 and in the sentences for remembering the order of transpositions, the C's at both ends are not emphasized. The reason is that no sharps or flats are used when the key is C natural, and that the keys of C♯ and C♭ are not often used. Also remind the students of the one letter in each series that is different from the rest: the letter F. A key signature of one flat indicates the key of F, whereas the other signatures made of flats all indicate flatted key tones. Something similar applies to F♯ in comparison with the other signatures made of sharps.

The use of sentences is the most common means by which the order of transposition is remembered, but a better way is to drill until one knows the key just by looking at the key signature. The sentences in the pupil text are intended more as a reinforcement of the order than as the method to be used each time the key of a song is found. So you are strongly urged to continue flash-card drill of the key signatures.

Writing key signatures, however, does not need nearly so much drill because it is needed only in writing music, not in singing. Teaching and practice are given so that the students become somewhat familiar with how it is done, but they need not be expected to learn how to write all the key signatures from memory. They will do well if they remember how to write only the key signatures for G and F on both the G clef and the F clef staffs.

Assign exercise 15 and the questions at the end of chapter 4 as written work, and tell the students to prepare for a chapter test.

Conducting the Singing Period

Drill with the fifth and sixth pages of sight-reading exercises. Demonstrate the importance of singing in the right key by starting a few of the suggested hymns just one step too high or too low. Suggestions:

"He Hideth My Soul" (510) (Try the key of E.)

"O Father, Lead Us" (491) (Try the key of A♭.)

"Blessed Be the Name" (3) (How does this hymn sound in the keys of G and B?)

Observe that in the last hymn above, the highest note in the soprano part is *Fa* and the lowest is *Sol.* The range of tones is considerably wider in the second hymn—from a low *Do* to a *Sol* in the next higher octave.

Quiz Questions

1. What are two differences between transposition by fifths and transposition by fourths? (Any two: *the order of the keys is reversed, one group of key signature is made of sharps and the other of flats, most key tones in one group are natural and most in the other group are flatted.*)

2. What sentence helps us to remember the order of transposition—
   a. when the key signature is made of sharps? *(Good deeds are ever bearing fruit.)*
   b. when the key signature is made of flats? *(Fruits borne early are delightfully good.)*

3. Where do you place a sharp to show the key of G? a flat to show the key of F? *(On line F; on line B.)*

Lesson 19

Review of Chapter Four

Teaching the Lesson

Use the quiz questions to review chapter 4, and the flash cards to review instant key recognition. Then give the chapter test.

Conducting the Singing Period

Review selections from the first six sight-reading drills. Have the students name the key of each hymn you sing; perhaps they can also sound the key tones on a pitch pipe. Suggestions:
"I Gave My Life for Thee"
"There Is No Name So Sweet on Earth" (22)
"Footprints of Jesus" (508)
"God's Way Is Best" (389)
"Standing on the Promises" (474)
Observe the pupils' singing to obtain singing grades.

Quiz Questions

1. What is a key? a key signature? *(A family of tones with a fixed relationship to its key tone; a group of sharps or flats that indicates the key.)*
2. Name two kinds of transposition. *(Transposition by fifths and by fourths.)*
3. What must be done to the key signature each time the key is transposed? *(A new sharp or flat must be added.)*
4. Why is the key of C called the natural key? *(None of its tones are sharped or flatted.)*
5. What is the order of transposition by fifths? by fourths? *(G, D,*

51

A, E, B, F♯; F, B♭, E♭, A♭, D♭, G♭)

6. Why do we say that transpositions move in a cycle? *(They begin with C and come back to C.)*

Lesson 20

Note and Rest Values, and Characters That Affect Note Values

Teaching the Lesson

The system of time value used in music is closely related to the system by which inches, yards, pounds, and miles are often divided into smaller parts. Each part is divided in half until the desired precision is obtained. In music, notes of varying time values are what produce the rhythm patterns with which we are familiar in the songs we sing. You could tap out the patterns for several songs and see whether the pupils can identify the songs to which they belong. (List the titles on the board for them to choose from.)

Time values in music are all relative. The different kinds of notes do have fixed relationships to each other, but they do not have absolute lengths comparable to absolute pitches because there is no generally accepted standard by which to define them. Indeed, such a standard is not even desirable because of the restriction it would place upon the speed of the singing. Thus the nonexistence of an absolute standard is a definite advantage; it frees us to sing each line of a song at a tempo which is the best suited to its message. See chapter 6 for more details on tempo.

The students are probably familiar with most of the characters which alter time value; be sure they also learn all the correct pronunciations. The tie is sometimes used when one stanza of a song has two syllables at a certain place but another stanza has only one (as in the first score of "Will Your Anchor Hold?"). The same thing commonly happens where there is a slur, as in the third score of the same song.

53

A dotted note is often followed immediately by a note of lesser time value; this produces a "skipping" rhythm pattern such as that in the song "His Way With Thee." The smaller note is needed to fill out each measure because of the extra time which the dot adds to the preceding note. In the song just mentioned, each combination of one dotted eighth note and one sixteenth note can be replaced by two eighth notes, and the timing still comes out right. But there is a definite change in the rhythm pattern.

The hold is the only one of the seven characters that is optional, and it is the only one that actually changes the timing of a song. Interestingly, however, many singers observe holds but ignore staccato marks, probably because they understand the former but not the latter. So make sure your students understand as well as observe both kinds of characters.

Your pupils will best understand the effect of triplets by singing a few songs that have a number of them. Then they will have the feel of triplets that one must have when he meets triplets in a new song. Show by beating time that the three notes of a triplet are sung with one sweep of the hand. Those three notes are usually eighth notes sung in the same amount of time as one quarter note.

Assign exercise 16 for written work.

Conducting the Singing Period

Sing a few scores of sight-reading exercises from the twelfth and thirteenth drills. Point out the rests and the characters that affect note values in the hymns you sing. Suggestions:

"Fairest Lord Jesus" (565) (Observe the half rest.)

"Jesus, Lover of My Soul" (Note the triplets, the dotted notes, and the slurs.)

"Will Your Anchor Hold?" (483) (Observe the ties and the holds.)

"His Way With Thee" (277) (The dotted notes produce a distinctive rhythm pattern.)

"Tread Softly" (Observe the staccato marks.)

"Be Ready When He Comes" (285) (This hymn has a pattern of double-dotted notes.)

Quiz Questions

1. When we speak of value in music, what kind of value are we

referring to? *(Time value.)*

2. What is the relationship between each note or rest and the next larger one? *(The smaller note or rest always has half the value of the next larger one.)*

3. What musical character is used—
   a. to indicate that a note is to be sung longer than its normal value, as the song leader directs? *(The hold, or fermata.)*
   b. to indicate that two notes should be sung as one? *(The tie.)*
   c. to indicate that the note should be sung in a slightly detached manner? *(The semistaccato mark.)*
   d. to indicate that the singer should slide from one pitch to another? *(The slur.)*
   e. to increase the value of a note by one-half? *(The dots.)*

4. How should three notes be sung if they have a *3* above or below them? *(They should be sung in the same time as two notes of the same value, or in one motion of the song leader's hand.)*

5. How much value does a second dot add to a dotted note? *(Half the value of the first dot.)*

Lesson 21

Repeat Signs

Teaching the Lesson

The students have been observing the musical characters taught in this lesson ever since they began to sing, for they learned to sing simply by imitating others. Thus they have repeated certain parts of some songs simply because they have never heard the songs sung any other way. This lesson teaches the pupils to observe repeat signs intelligently rather than through the mere force of habit. Then they will also know what to do when they meet these signs in a new song.

Observe the difference in the two reasons for which repeat signs are used. One is simple necessity; the other results from the desire to achieve a specific end. These two reasons apply to just about everything that we do in life, and especially to singing. Some people sing of necessity, because they are asked to do so or because everyone else in the group is singing. Others sing for a specific purpose—to glorify God, to edify and encourage others, to redeem the time, to express the joy in their hearts. For which purpose do *we* sing?

Point out that repeat dots are sometimes overlooked, probably because dots can also be used after notes to give them added length and above notes to indicate the semistaccato style. But often there are other clues given as well, which help to make such an oversight less likely. One example is the "repeat p" printed above the second and fourth scores of "Shall You? Shall I?"

Assign exercise 17 for written work. Continue to give occasional flash-card drill on the key signatures so that the students' skill in identifying them stays sharp.

Conducting the Singing Period

Sing selected exercises from the first six and the twelfth and thirteenth pages of sight-reading drills. Sing hymns in which various types of repeats are found. Suggestions:

"We Now Have Met to Worship Thee" (54)

"Shall You? Shall I?" (291)

"Where He Leads I'll Follow" (494)

"Tell Me the Story of Jesus" (317)

"Give Me the Bible" (138)

Quiz Questions

1. When can a music writer save space by using a repeat? *(When the ending of a song uses music found earlier in the song.)*
2. What is another reason for the use of repeats? *(To emphasize a certain part of a song.)*
3. When are repeat dots used? *When a portion of the music is simply to be repeated.)*
4. In repeats with first and second endings, what is done with the first ending when the music is sung the second time? *(It is omitted.)*
5. Explain the meanings of the abbreviations D.C. and D.S. *(D.C. means* da capo *and instructs the singer to repeat from the beginning of the song. D.S. means* dal segno *and instructs the singer to repeat from segno.)*

Lesson 22

Pulse—Unit of Measure

Teaching the Lesson

It has already been pointed out that in music there is no absolute unit of measure for the length of tones. But there is a relative unit—the pulse. The concept of the pulse should be simple for the students to understand because they all know what a pulse is in a physical sense. Lengths of notes and rests are determined by the number of pulses they receive, with the pulse note one pulse long and each other kind as long as its value in relation to the pulse note.

Obviously a person must have a good comprehension of fractional relationships if he expects to understand the relationship among notes of differing values. So if your students show any weakness in understanding fractions, give some instruction in that area so that they can better grasp the relationships among different kinds of notes. (It is helpful to compare notes to the various fractions of an inch on a ruler.) The reverse approach can also help your pupils to do better with fractions. If they understand by the study of pulses that two quarter notes are equal to one half note, for example, they will have a broader concept of the relationship between two-fourths and one-half.

A measure, by its simplest definition, is the amount of music from one bar to the next. But here again there is much more involved than simply dividing the staff into segments of a specified length. Each measure must include a specified number of *pulses,* whether it takes one note or ten to equal that number. Some songs have only two or three measures per score whereas others have as many as eight measures in a score of the same length.

Figure 75 is closely related to the subject of the next lesson—the time signature. The upper number of the time signature indicates the kind of measure: 2 for two-pulse measures, 3 for three-pulse measure, and so forth. See "Conducting the Singing Period" for a suggestion on how to demonstrate the number of pulses in different measures.

Assign exercise 18 for written work.

Conducting the Singing Period

Sing selected scores from the sight-reading drills of two-, three-, and four-pulse measures (numbers 7-9). After the pupils are familiar with them, try singing the notes and counting the pulses in each measure rather than saying the syllable names. Sing "one, two, three" with three-pulse measures, for example, applying numbers to notes according to their values. You could do the same with a few of the suggested hymns. Suggestions:

"When I Survey the Wondrous Cross" (113)

"Prince of Peace, Control My Will" (421) (Point out that some measures contain only one note.)

"Ever Lead Me" (502)

"Oh, How I Love Jesus" (46) (Observe that this hymn begins with a divided measure.)

Quiz Questions

1. What is the smallest unit of time measurement in music? What is the next larger unit? *(The pulse; the measure.)*
2. Why do we call the note the timepiece in music? *(The note shows how long a tone is to be sung.)*
3. Suppose the half note is the pulse note. How many pulses long would a whole note be? A quarter note? *(Two pulses; one-half pulse.)*
4. How can it be shown that each measure in a song is of equal time value? *(By counting the pulses in each measure.)*

Lesson 23

The Time Signature

Teaching the Lesson

The time signature is another example of the order and efficiency in music notation. A note shows both pitch and length in one symbol, and the time signature is also one symbol that shows two things. It is true that the singer could determine for himself what kind of measures the music consists of and which kind of note is probably the pulse note. But it is better for the composer to decide these things and indicate with an appropriate time signature his intention for the timing of the song.

The time signature looks like a fraction, and it can also be thought of in terms of a fraction. It can be considered the total time value that is contained in each measure. For if each measure in $\frac{3}{4}$ timing has three pulses and the quarter note is the pulse note, each measure will have the value of the time signature—$\frac{3}{4}$. Each measure in $\frac{4}{4}$ timing is equal in length to four quarter notes, which have a combined value of one (a whole note). Further, if a measure in $\frac{3}{4}$ timing consists of three quarter notes, it is called primitive; if it has other kinds of notes that total $\frac{3}{4}$, it is called derivative.

Observe that a number of time signatures are equal in value; $\frac{3}{4}$ and $\frac{6}{8}$ provide one example. The reason for the use of both is suggested in the lesson—we tend to sing quarter notes more slowly than eighth notes. Thus the time signature is also a general indicator as to how fast a song should be sung. Another indicator sometimes used is a metronomic number, which gives a suggested number of pulses per minute. But it takes a metronome to measure out the pulses if one wishes to achieve accuracy in observing metronomic numbers.

Assign exercise 19 for written work.

Conducting the Singing Period

Use the first page of divided beats (tenth sight-reading exercise) for drill with this lesson. Sing hymns with differing time signatures. Suggestions:

"Thou Art the Way" (341)

"Oh, Beautiful Star of Bethlehem" (95)

"Ready to Do His Will" (401)

"He Was Nailed to the Cross for Me" (107)

"Walk in the Light" (450) (Observe the timing changes in the last three hymns.)

Remind the pupils to sing with good expression and at an appropriate tempo and volume.

Quiz Questions

1. What does the numerator of a time signature show? the denominator? *(The number of pulses per measure; which kind of note is the pulse note.)*
2. How many different time signatures are used? *(Fifteen.)*
3. Which three kinds of notes are used as pulse notes? *(The half note, the quarter note, and the eighth note.)*
4. Why is the half note not used as the pulse note in six-, nine-, and 12-pulse measures? *(We tend to sing half notes slowly but six-, nine-, and twelve-pulse music more quickly. Because of this conflict, the half note is not used as the pulse note in these measures.)*
5. What kind of measures—
   a. have notes of different values? *(Derivative measures.)*
   b. are made of pulse notes only? *(Primitive measures.)*
6. How would a primitive measure in $\frac{6}{4}$ timing be constructed? *(With six quarter notes.)*

Lesson 24

Checking the Measure

Teaching the Lesson

If each measure in a song has the number of pulses indicated by the time signature, then it is logical to expect the sum of the notes and rests in each measure to equal the time signature. In 3/4 timing, for example, many measures have three quarter notes—the total of which is $\frac{3}{4}$. Thus we find that this lesson naturally follows the two preceding ones. Adding notes is also taught in *Growing in Music,* Book One of this series, but dotted notes are not included.

If the pupils check measures in actual music, however, they may find that the first measure does not always seem to agree with the time signature. The reason is that sometimes a measure is split between the end of one stanza and the beginning of the next. In such a case it will be found that the last and the first measures together add up to the time signature.

In this lesson, notes can again be related to fractions. Unlike fractions cannot be added until they are changed to fractions with common denominators, and unlike notes cannot be added either. A note of a smaller value must always be added to another note of equal value before it can be combined with a note of greater value.

In connection with figure 81, ask this question: What time signatures could be used with measures having these total values? $\frac{2}{2}$ or $\frac{4}{4}$, and $\frac{3}{2}$, $\frac{6}{4}$, or $\frac{12}{8}$.) The measures that are not true in figure 82 are these: first score, second and last measures; second score, first and fourth measures.

Assign exercise 20 for written work.

Conducting the Singing Period

Drill with the second page of divided beats (eleventh sight-reading exercise). Point out some measures that are primitive and some that are derivative in the hymns you sing. Suggestions:

"I Wonder, Often Wonder" (30)

"We'll Work Till Jesus Comes" (203)

"Close to Thee" (These measures are all derivative.)

"Onward, Christian Soldiers" (The many primitive measures create a "marching" rhythm.)

Quiz Questions

1. What musical character indicates the sum that the notes in each measure should total? *(The time signature.)*
2. Which notes should be added first? *(The notes of the smallest values.)*
3. What must be done with an eighth note before it can be added to a quarter note? *(It must be combined with another eighths note.)*
4. What kind of answer will be obtained when all the notes of each measure in a song are added? *(The answer will be one note, which will be the same for all the measures in the song.)*

Lesson 25

Beating Patterns and Accent

Teaching the Lesson

Beating time is done so that singers can see the pulses of music. It is a skill that song leaders must develop, but the singers must also understand its significance so that they can follow the song leader intelligently. The song leader must develop his skill by practicing in private so that he can concentrate on the words when he leads songs in public worship services. Otherwise the beating of time will become mechanical and will detract from the message of the song.

Emphasize that each motion of the hand always indicates either one or three pulses, never two or four. If this rule requires very rapid hand motions, the song is probably being sung too fast. Remember, the time signature is one indicator of how fast the song should be sung.

The beating patterns of figure 84 are useful in understanding pulses and seeing how they are related to measures. But since many people find them distracting in actual song leading, a simple down-up pattern is much more common, even among professional conductors. The song leader should still be aware of accent, however, and show the most heavily accented pulses with downward motions of his hand.

Once the beating of time for a song has begun, the rhythm of the motions does not usually need to be interrupted except at an occasional phrase bar and at the end of each stanza. The only other place where a song leader should temporarily suspend his hand motions is at a hold—unless he wishes to indicate precisely how long he desires the hold to be sung. Too many singers interrupt the rhythm at the end of every short phrase and then start over with the next phrase.

In connection with accent, be sure to make it clear that there is only one strong (primary) accent in each measure, but there may be more than one secondary accent. In $\frac{9}{8}$ timing, for example, the first pulse receives the primary accent, the fourth and seventh pulses receive secondary accents, and all the remaining pulses are unaccented.

Have you been drilling instant key recognition occasionally? Assign exercise 21 and the questions at the end of chapter 5 for written work, and tell the pupils to study for a test on chapter 5.

Conducting the Singing Period

Use numbers 7-9, 14, and 15 of the sight-reading exercises to drill the various beating patterns. You could also begin teaching how to lead songs: have various students determine the key and sound the correct key tone as was taught in chapter 4, and then they can beat time as is taught in this lesson. Suggested hymns:

"Keep Me Near Thee" (506) $\frac{2}{4}$ timing

"Not All the Blood of Beasts" (109) $\frac{3}{2}$ timing

"No Friend Like Jesus" (526) $\frac{4}{4}$ timing

"Just As Seemeth Good to Thee" (493) $\frac{6}{8}$ timing

"I Will Sing of My Redeemer" (8) $\frac{9}{8}$ and $\frac{12}{8}$ timing

Quiz Questions

1. What is a beat? *(A motion of the song leader's hand.)*
2. When each beat indicates one pulse, what kind of measures are being sung? *(Simple measures.)*
3. Each beat may also indicate how many pulses? What kind of measures are being sung then? *(Three; compound measures.)*
4. How many beating patterns are there? Demonstrate them. *(Three; pupils' demonstrations should coincide with the patterns illustrated in the lesson.)*
5. When is the down beat made? The up beat? *(Immediately after the measure bar; just before the next measure bar.)*
6. Which pulse in all measures is the strongest? *(The first pulse.)*
7. What are the strong pulses called? *(Accented pulses.)*

Lesson 26

Review of Chapter Five

Teaching the Lesson

Review the chapter by asking the quiz questions. Then give the chapter 5 test.

Conducting the Singing Period

Review selections from numbers 7-15 of the sight-reading drills. Sing hymns of different timing patterns and have the students beat time. Suggestions:

"My Faith Looks Up to Thee" (453) $\frac{2}{2}$ *timing*

"Give Me Jesus" (270) $\frac{3}{4}$ *timing*

"I Would Not Have My Way" (393) $\frac{4}{4}$ *timing*

"Long Have They Waited" (214) $\frac{6}{4}$ *timing*

"Blessed Assurance" (477) $\frac{9}{8}$ timing

Quiz Questions

1. What kind of musical character is used—
   a. to increase the value of a note by one-half? *(A dot.)*
   b. to indicate that three notes should be sung in one beat? *(A triplet.)*
   c. to show that a note should be sung longer, as the song leader directs? *(A hold.)*
2. What are two reasons for the use of repeats? *(To save space and to give added emphasis.)*
3. What is the word that indicates the end of a repeated part? *(Fine.)*
4. What is a pulse note? *(A note that is one pulse long.)*

66

5. Why do we say that all the measures in a song are of equal length? *(They all have the same number of pulses.)*

6. What two things does the time signature show? *(The number of pulses in each measure and which note is the pulse note.)*

7. What is a primitive measure? What is the other kind of measure called? *(A measure constructed of pulse notes only; a derivative measure.)*

8. How can measures be checked to see that they are made correctly? *(The notes can be added to see whether they total the value indicated by the time signature.)*

9. What is the value of beating time? *(It helps the singers to sense the rhythm and stay together.)*

10. An accented pulse may be followed by how many unaccented pulses? *(One or two.)*

Lesson 27

Observing the Mood and the Message, and Tempo

Teaching the Lesson

This chapter treats the department of music called dynamics, which is mentioned in chapter 1 as the most neglected of the three departments. One reason for the neglect is that music alters the natural pitch and stress that we place upon words in normal speech. Another is perhaps because of a negative reaction to people who put exaggerated expression into their singing, and a third is because of a habit of singing without thinking about the words. All these hindrances can be overcome by concentrating on the words and considering honestly how they should be sung for maximum expression.

Authors and composers do attempt to give directions for proper expression by the use of various words and symbols, but these can never take the place of paying careful attention to the words. The discussion on how "Silent Night" should be sung makes it plain that such directions are simply too general to apply to every phrase of a song. Only as we sing in the same way that we talk (as much as possible) can we do justice to the profound thoughts expressed in many of our hymns.

Yet it is good to know the meanings of the terms that give direction to tempo; for if singers do not understand them, they may fall into the habit of singing at a tempo that is not at all appropriate for the hymn. Therefore, drill the terms that are listed in figure 90, giving pointers to help the students remember their meanings. *Moderato* and *presto* should present little trouble, and *andante* should not be difficult either if it is associated with walking. That leaves only *adagio* and *allegro*, which we can remember by pronouncing them at different speeds. Drag out *adagio*, but pronounce *allegro* with speed and vigor.

The need for expressive singing is one reason for which we have song leaders. It is their responsibility to guide the audience in giving proper expression to the words by singing at an appropriate tempo, at a proper volume, and in a fitting style. Since you, the teacher, are the song leader in your class, it is your duty to effect proper expression whenever your students sing together.

Assign exercise 22 for written work.

Conducting the Singing Period

Practice with the sight-reading drills may be continued as you desire. In this singing period, emphasize good expression and pay special attention to proper tempo. Suggested hymns:

"Silent Night"

"Glorious Things of Thee Are Spoken"

"He Loves Me"

"Weighed in the Balance" (294)

Quiz Questions

1. Why should a singer pay close attention to the words when he is singing? *(So that he can sing with proper expression.)*
2. Changes made in the speed, volume, and style of speaking or singing are called what? *(Voice modulations.)*
3. What is tempo? *(The speed of singing.)*
4. What is indicated by the term—
    a. allegro? *(Fast tempo.)*
    b. ritardando? *(Gradually slower.)*
    c. andante? *(Slow tempo.)*
    d. accelerando? *(Gradually faster.)*
    e. moderato? *(Moderate tempo.)*
5. When is the direction *a tempo* given? *(After a direction to increase or decrease tempo, indicated by* accelerando *or* ritardando.)

Lesson 28

Volume and Style

Teaching the Lesson

Since music alters the normal expression that is put into speech, you and your pupils should find it enlightening to read the words of several songs as they would be read if they were prose. ("Tread Softly" and "Onward, Christian Soldiers" are two good choices.) Where does the voice naturally become louder or softer? Where do you tend to read faster or slower? Reading the lines as prose is even more instructive than reading them as poetry, for the rhythm of poetry also tends to decrease expression. Such a reading is an excellent guide in determining when the singing should be done softly, loudly, rapidly, or slowly.

The terms and symbols that give direction to volume are somewhat more simple than are those pertaining to tempo. Actually, there are only three different terms used in figure 92; the other four directions are variations and combinations of the three basic terms. *Crescendo* can be associated with *increase,* and *decrescendo* or *diminuendo* with *decrease* or *diminish.* And the term *swell,* in addition to the symbols in figure 93, is essentially self-explanatory.

You will have to judge from your own pupils' singing habits whether to emphasize more volume or less, faster singing or slower. Since the tendency in the middle grades is to sing with little enthusiasm, you will probably need to strive for more volume rather than less. Remember that the students' attitude toward singing is often a reflection of their teacher's attitude. So strive first for a positive, enthusiastic outlook on your own part. Few persons are able to resist becoming inspired if their leader is inspired.

But again, avoid emphasizing volume, tempo, or style to the point that they detract from the message of the song. Since music is only the vehicle on which a message is carried, the words must always be the most impressive element in our singing. No message must ever be lost because of the way in which it is presented.

Assign exercise 23 for written work, and tell the students to prepare for a test on chapters 4-6.

Conducting the Singing Period

Continue to emphasize expressive singing, giving direction to tempo, volume, and style. Suggested hymns:
"Tread Softly"
"Onward, Christian Soldiers"
"The Eventide Falls Gently Now" (110)
"Awake, Awake, O Earth"
"I Love to Steal Awhile Away"
"One Day!" (309)

Quiz Questions

1. In relation to tempo and volume, what is a common tendency in singing? *(A common tendency is to sing too fast and too loud.)*
2. What are the three main terms used to give direction to volume? What do they mean? *(The three main terms are* piano, mezzo, *and* forte; *they mean softly, "half voice" or medium, and loudly.)*
3. What is the meaning of the term—
   a. diminuendo? *(Gradually softer.)*
   b. crescendo? *(Gradually louder.)*
   c. swell? *(Gradually louder, then gradually softer.)*
   d. decrescendo? *(Gradually softer.)*
4. Name the style that is—
   a. strongly accented. *(Marcato.)*
   b. very choppy. *(Staccato.)*
   c. smooth and gentle. *(Legato.)*
   d. somewhat detached. *(Semistaccato.)*
5. How can we be the most effective in singing expressively? *(We can try to sense the message and the general feeling of a song.)*

Lesson 29

Review of Chapters Four to Six

Teaching the Lesson

Use the quiz questions for review before giving the test. Tell the students to be ready for a book-length test by the next music class.

Conducting the Singing Period

Have several of the students lead a few hymns, giving direction to proper expression and beating time as they have learned. Suggestions:

"My Saviour's Love" (24)
"The Ninety-Nine" (202)
"Stepping in the Light" (561)
"'Tis Midnight" (114)

Quiz Questions

1. What is a key? *(A family of tones with a fixed relationship to its key tone.)*
2. What is transposition by fifths? How are key signatures made for this kind of transposition? *(Choosing the fifth tone as the key tone of the new key; they are made of sharps.)*
3. Which key is the natural key? *(The key of C.)*
4. What must be remembered about the key tones in transposition by fourths? Which letter is an exception? *(The key tones are flatted instead of natural; the letter F.)*
5. Which musical character—
   a. increases the value of a note by one-half? *(A dot.)*
   b. shows that two notes should be sung as one? *(A tie.)*
   c. marks a note that is to be sung longer than usual, at the song

73

leader's direction? *(A hold or fermata.)*

6. What are the words for which D.C. stands? What does this direction mean? *(D.C. stands for* da capo; *it means to repeat from the beginning of the song.)*

7. How is each measure in a song equal in length? *(Each has the same number of pulses and is of equal time value.)*

8. All the notes in each measure should add up to the value indicated by what? *(The time signature.)*

9. How often should the song leader complete the beating pattern? *(He should complete it for each measure.)*

10. What is an important rule to remember—
    a. about proper tempo? *(It must not be too slow or too fast; it must change gradually rather than suddenly.)*
    b. about proper volume? *(It should be medium, with variations to loudness and softness as the words suggest.)*
    c. about proper style? *(Each style must be used only at certain places within hymns; one style must not be used continuously.)*

Lesson 30

Book-length Review

Teaching the Lesson

Use the quiz questions for review; then give the final test.

Conducting the Singing Period

Continue to give direction to enthusiastic, expressive singing. Again have a few of the students lead songs. Suggestions:

"To Thy Pastures, Fair and Large" (485)
"Pass Me Not, O Gentle Saviour" (380)
"Christ Arose" (119)
"Dare to Be a Daniel" (563)

Quiz Questions

1. What are two good purposes of singing? *(To worship the Lord, to encourage ourselves and others, to redeem the time, etc.)*
2. Name the three departments of music. *(Rhythmics, melodics, and dynamics.)*
3. Why do we need two staffs for the music of our hymns? *(So that there is room for the notes of all four singing parts—soprano, alto, tenor, and bass.)*
4. What unit of measure is used to define absolute pitch? *(Vibrations per second.)*
5. Name the three types of scales and give a noteworthy characteristic of each one. *(Major diatonic scale—it is the scale most commonly used. Minor diatonic scale—it has a unique mood. Chromatic scale—it consists of all half steps.)*
6. How is the ascending chromatic scale different from the

descending chromatic scale? *(The vowels in the chromatic tones are different.)*

7. How is transposition by fifths different from transposition by fourths? *(The key signatures are made of sharps versus flats; the order of the transpositions are opposite; the key tones are natural versus flatted.)*

8. How do transpositions move in a cycle? *They begin with C and come back to C.*

9. What are two reasons for the use of repeats? *(To save space and to give added emphasis.)*

10. How are primitive and derivative measures different from each other? *(Primitive measures contain pulse notes only; derivative measures contain notes other than pulse notes, but their total value always agrees with the time signature.)*

11. What is an accented pulse? *(A pulse that is stronger than other pulses, which are unaccented.)*

12. What is meant by expressive singing? *(Singing that expresses the message of a song in the most effective way possible.)*

Answer Section

Study Questions Answer Key
Workbook Answer Key
Test Booklet Answer Key

Study Questions Answer Key

Chapter One

1. God's people should use their voices to praise the Lord and to edify and encourage themselves and others. Singing is one excellent way to do this.
2. Singing should also be an experience from the heart.
3. Two Bible references to singing not mentioned in the text are 2 Samuel 6 and 2 Chronicles 20. (Other answers possible.)
4. Another name for the voice box is the *larynx.*
5. The vocal cords are like narrow ribbons.
6. The vocal cords are open when you whisper.
7. The three departments of music are *melodics, rhythmics,* and *dynamics.*
8. A whole rest would be studied in the department of *rhythmics.*
9. The symbol ⁴⁄₄ would be studied in the department of *rhythmics.*
10. The department of *dynamics* is most likely to be neglected.

Chapter Two

1. The short, added lines are called *ledger lines.* They are added to make more degrees than are on the staff alone.
2. Three clef signatures are used: the *G clef,* the *F clef,* and the *C clef.*
3. The *G clef* names the second line G.
4. Pitch is absolute so that the symbols in music have definite meanings. Absolute pitch is the very core and backbone of melodics.
5. *Sharps, flats,* and *naturals* are used as accidentals.
6. A natural only lowers the pitch when it cancels the effect of a sharp. If it cancels the effect of a flat, a natural *raises* the pitch.
7. Possible answer:

    G   G♯   G

8. Space E is a half step less than an octave higher because an accidental affects only the degree upon which it is placed.

Chapter Three

1. The three scales in common use are the *major diatonic scale,* the *minor diatonic scale,* and the *chromatic scale.*
2. The diatonic scale has some whole-step and some half-step intervals; the chromatic scale has only half-step intervals. The diatonic scale has eight tones; the chromatic scale has thirteen tones.
3. We find half-step intervals between the third and fourth tones and between the seventh and eighth tones.
4. The moods are different. Also, the home tones are different.
5. We find the half-step intervals between the second and third tones and between the fifth and sixth tones of the minor diatonic scale.
6. The three moods of the minor scale are *sad, majestic,* and *terrible.*
7. We can add chromatic tones between the tones that are separated by whole-step intervals.
8. The syllables for the ascending chromatic scale are *Do, Di, Re, Ri, Mi, Fa, Fi, Sol, Si, La, Li, Ti, Do.* The syllables for the descending scale are *Do, Ti, Te, La, Le, Sol, Se, Fa Mi, Me, Re, Ra, Do.*
9.
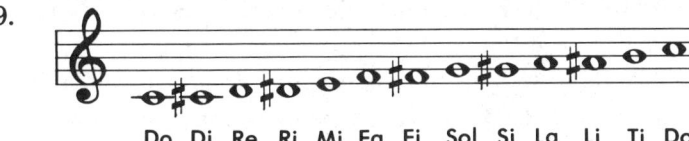

Do Di Re Ri Mi Fa Fi Sol Si La Li Ti Do

Chapter Four

1. A key is a family of tones with a fixed relationship to its key tone.
2. We can observe the pitch of the key tone. The pitch of the key tone is the name of the key.
3. Each transposition requires the addition of another sharp or flat to the key signature. So the number of sharps or flats in the key signature indicates the key.
4. We begin transpositions from the key of *C.*
5. The order of transposition by fifths is *G, D, A, E, B, F♯.*
6. The order of transposition by fourths is *F, B♭, E♭, A♭, D♭, G♭.*
7. The letters *F, C, G, D, A,* and *E* are sharped.
8. The letters *B, E, A, D, G,* and *C* are flatted.

Chapter Five

1. The five kinds of notes and rests are *whole* (○ ━), *half* (♩ ━),
   quarter (♩ ♪), *eighth* (♪ ♪), and *sixteenth* (♪ ♪).
2. The whole note is *one*, the half note is *one-half*, the quarter note
   is *one-fourth*, the eighth note is *one-eighth*, and the sixteenth note
   is *one-sixteenth*.
3. Five characters which temporarily affect the value of a note are
   the *tie*, the *slur*, the *dot*, the *hold*, the *triplet*, the *staccato mark*,
   and the *semistaccato mark* (any five of these seven). They are
   illustrated here.

| tie | slur | dot | hold | triplet | staccato mark | semistaccato mark |

4. The *pulse* is used to measure note value.
5. Seconds are to minutes as pulses are to *measures*.
6. The time signatures that could be used for a three-pulse measure
   are $\frac{3}{2}$, $\frac{3}{4}$, and $\frac{3}{8}$.
7. Yes, it is possible for a derivative measure in $\frac{3}{4}$ time to have three
   notes. It could have a half note and two eighth notes.
8. The total note value in $\frac{4}{4}$ time is one whole note per measure.
9. With a simple measure, the song leader uses one hand motion to
   indicate each pulse. With a compound measure, each hand motion
   indicates three pulses.
10. The time signatures which use the down-up beating pattern are $\frac{2}{2}$,
    $\frac{2}{4}$, $\frac{2}{8}$, $\frac{6}{4}$, and $\frac{6}{8}$.

Chapter Six

1. Expressive singing is singing that conveys the message of the
   words clearly and effectively.
2. The speed of a song is called the *tempo*.
3. *Presto* indicates very fast singing; *adagio* indicates very slow
   singing.
4. You would not likely find *a tempo* following *allegro* because *allegro*
   gives direction to the general tempo at which the entire song should
   be sung. *A tempo*, which is a direction to return to the original
   tempo, only follows *ritardando* or *accelerando*.

5. *Tempo* is the speed of singing. *A tempo* is a direction to return to the original speed after singing gradually faster or slower.

6. ⟨══ *crescendo*—Sing gradually louder.
   ══⟩ *decrescendo* or *diminuendo*—Sing gradually softer.
   ⟨══⟩ *swell*—Sing gradually louder, then gradually softer.

7. *Legato* is a smooth and gentle style. *Staccato* is a choppy style in which each note is sung for only one-fourth of its time value. *Semistaccato* is a detached style in which each note is sung for one-half of its time value. *Marcato* is a strongly accented style.

8. The most important factor for expressive singing is putting forth a personal effort to understand the message of each song, then singing in such a way that the message is expressed in the most effective way possible.

Note: Suggested song numbers are given in brackets. All song numbers given are from the *Church Hymnal* unless otherwise indicated.

Lesson 1
Chapter 1, pp. 11–13
Music Is Important; The Human Voice

1. (Sample answers.) Wind in the trees, locusts, rippling water, airplane, wood planer, drills, bells, buzzers, harvester, lawn mower
2. The music that is sung by men, women, and children, especially when it is an outpouring of their heart, is the most valuable.
3. (Sample answers.) breathing, walking, jogging, printing press, baler
4. Psalm 96:1. "O sing unto the Lord a new song: sing unto the Lord, all the earth."
   Psalm 98:1. "O sing unto the LORD a new song; for he hath done marvelous things: his right hand, and his holy arm, hath gotten him the victory."
   James 5:13 "Is any merry? let him sing songs."
   (What reference to Psalm 96:1 does Isaac Watts make in number 57 in the Church Hymnal? "Prepare new honors for his name, and songs before unknown.")
5. My soul, sing about God's wonderful love. He carefully watches over mankind from his bright, shining throne in heaven. He in mercy still is offering His grace to man. He has made heaven and earth, and everything moves at His command. We are as nothing compared to God's greatness, so why would God show us so much love.
6. a. trachea   b. larynx   c. epiglottis   d. cartilage
7. When air passes through tightened bands, called vocal cords, they vibrate, making a sound. *(The more air there is, the louder the sound is. The tighter the vocal cords are, the higher the pitch is.)*
8. (Any two.) Do not force a husky voice; instead, relax it.
   Avoid very loud singing or speaking, especially if it becomes painful.
   Do not continually strain the voice by going to extreme ends of the scale, especially boys trying to sing bass. (Boys should not try to sing low bass before their voices mature.)
   If the voice is affected by a cold, do not force it or overuse it.

Lesson 2
Chapter 1, pp. 13–15
System of Study; Frances R. Havergal

1. rhythmics, melodics, dynamics

2. a. dynamics b. melodics c. dynamics d. rhythmics
3. a. rhythmics   d. dynamics   g. rhythmics
   b. melodics   e. melodics   h. dynamics
   c. melodics   f. rhythmics   i. rhythmics
4. Frances R. Havergal learned five languages: French, German, Greek, Hebrew, and Latin. She memorized the entire New Testament and Isaiah and Psalms.

Note: The exercises labeled *Extra* include material the students have not studied yet this year. If you use them, the students may need some additional assistance. Some of these are included on tests, where they are also labeled *Extra.*

Extra

5. a. C   e. A   h. D   k. E
   b. G♭   f. E♭   i. A♭   l. B♭
   c. F   g. B   j. G   m. D♭
   d. F♯

Lesson 3

Chapter 1, pp. 11–14
Review

1. musical   6. cartilage   11. melodics
2. rhythm   7. vocal cords   12. b
3. teach   8. rhythmics   13. a, b, d
4. admonish   9. Dynamics   14. d
5. larynx   10. voice culture   15. c

Extra

16. a. G♭   c. F♯   e. B
    b. E   d. D♭

17.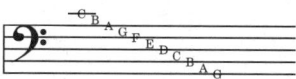

Lesson 4

Chapter 2, pp. 17–19
Introduction to the Staff; Clef Signatures

1. a. ledger lines
   b. degrees
   c. clef
   d. nine
   e. grand staff

2. The staff is made of five lines and four spaces.

3. The staff is used to represent pitch. When a note is placed on the staff, it has the pitch of the degree on which it is placed.

4. a. G clef
   b. soprano, alto
   c. F clef
   d. tenor, bass
   e. C clef
   f. tenor in men's music (first and second tenor)

5. The G clef and the C clef are lettered alike.

6. Middle C   C clef   F clef   G clef   ledger line   brace

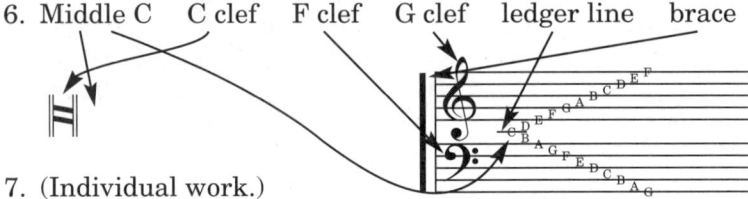

7. (Individual work.)

Lesson 5

Chapter 2, pp. 20–21
Absolute Pitch; The Function of Accidentals

1. A pitch is determined by the number of vibrations per second (vps). *(For each octave the vibrations per second exactly doubles.)*

2. absolute pitch

3. The pitch pipe gives the leader absolute pitch, enabling him to use the same pitch the composer had in mind when he wrote the music. *(Some people are tone perfect without an instrument.)*

4. a. sharp
   b. double sharp
   c. natural
   d. accidentals
   e. flat
   f. double flat

5. a. natural
   b. double flat
   c. flat
   d. sharp
   e. double sharp

6. They are not used on the degrees that are sharped or flatted in the key signature.

7. (Individual work.)

Lesson 6

Chapter 2, pp. 21–23
Naturals; Double Sharps and Double Flats

1. A natural cancels a sharp or flat that is in the key signature, or a sharp or flat of a previous note in the same measure.

2. If the key signature is made of sharps, the second note is Le. If the key signature is made of flats, the second note is Li.

3. A double sharp is never found in a song when the key signature is made of flats.

A double flat is never found in a song when the key signature is made of sharps.

4. a. raises the note one-half step
    b. lowers the note one-half step
    c. raises the note one-half step
    d. raises the note one-half step

5. a (Di) and b (Ra) *(Technically the Di is a bit lower than Ra. We don't make a difference, but a few singers and musical instruments do.)*

6.

7.

Review

8.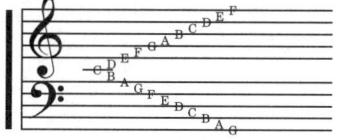

Songs with Accidentals

[227] Last score—The natural cancels the key signature. Note that the following flat returns the degree to it's flatted pitch.

[638] Shows that a measure bar cancels the effect of an accidental. Also note the progression of tenor on the last score as they follow the accidentals. On which two notes with accidentals will they sing the same pitch? Why did the composer use a sharp before a Sol one time and a flat before a La the next time?

[212] The flat for soprano in the middle of the second score should be a double flat.

[150, 583] Double sharp

[455] Note the flat in tenor. Which note does the flat effect?

[229] The natural is not really needed; the measure bar already canceled the effect of the accidental. The natural alerts the singer to this. But this poses a potential problem when the singer understands the effect of the measure bar; at first glance he isn't sure what to do with the natural.

Lesson 7
Chapter 2, pp. 24–27
Rules for the Use of Accidentals; Philip Paul Bliss

1. They can be canceled by a natural, or by a measure bar.
2. a. interval   b. steps
3. a. A double sharp should never be used with a key signature made of flats.
   b. The second La does not need a sharp; the first sharp is still in effect.
   c. The natural is not needed; the measure bar cancels the effect of the sharp.
4. a. E♯   c. G♯   e. A   g. A
   b. E♯   d. F   f. C
5.

   B♭   E   D   E

6. E–F; B–C
7. a. 1   c. 2   e. 1½
   b. 1   d. 0   f. ½
8. seven (five whole steps and two half steps)
9. Philip Paul Bliss gained inspiration for his hymns by traveling widely and by listening to many sermons.

Lesson 8
Chapter 2, pp. 17–26
Review

1. staff   5. grand staff   9. tenor   13. absolute
2. degrees   6. brace   10. bass   14. accidentals
3. ledger lines   7. Soprano   11. C clef   15. interval
4. clef   8. alto   12. pitch   16. steps
17. a. C   c. F   e. G
    b. B   d. F   f. C
18. when they are used in the key signature
19.   F-clef   C-clef   G-cleft

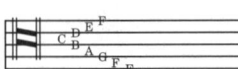   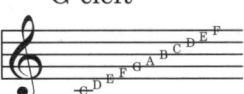

20. a. to cancel the effect of a sharp or flat on a previous note or in the time signature

b. to lower a degree ½ step when the degree was previously flatted in the key signature

c. to lower a degree ½ step

d. to raise a degree ½ step

e. to raise a degree ½ step when the degree was previously sharped by the key signature

21.

Lesson 9

Chapter 3, pp. 29–31
Introducing the Scale; Different Kinds of Scales

1. Fa, Re, Sol, Do, Mi, Ti, La, Do
2. a. scale   b. interval   c. diatonic   d. steps
3. I. Diatonic scale
   A. Major diatonic scale
   B. Minor diatonic scale
   II. Chromatic scale
4. The musical sounds must have order.
5. A diatonic scale has whole and half steps; a chromatic has all half-steps.
6. two *(The half steps must be there to make the chords sound right. To demonstrate, compare the Do–Mi–Si chord to the Do–Mi–Sol chord.)*

Extra

7. a. E♭   c. F♯   e. G♭   g. D
   b. F   d. D♭   f. E   h. B

Lesson 10

Chapter 3, pp. 31–35
The Major Diatonic Scale; The Minor Diatonic Scale Moods of the Diatonic Scale

1. Do, Re, Mi, Fa, Sol, La, Ti, Do   Major Diatonic Scale
2. La, Ti, Do, Re, Mi, Fa, Sol, La   Minor Diatonic Scale
3. a. home tone   b. octave   c. mood
4. (Any two.)
   They have the same syllable names.
   The half steps come between Mi–Fa and Ti–Do.
   Both have eight tones and seven intervals.
   Both have five whole steps and two half steps.

5. a. Major: 3–4; 7–8   Minor: 2–3; 5–6
   b. Major: Do   Minor: La
   c. Major: happiness, contentment
      Minor: sad, majestic, terrible
6. The chord of the first, third, and fifth tones
7. It creates strange feelings.
   It is often interpreted as being unpleasant because it is different from what we are used to. (It is possible, however, to develop appreciation for the rich harmony and expression in songs with minor tunes.)

Lesson 11

Chapter 3, pp. 35–39
The Chromatic Scale; Fanny Crosby

1. Di, Ri, Fi, Si, Li   Te, Le, Se, Me, Ra
2. a. chromatic tones   d. Do
   b. thirteen   e. vowel: i; pronunciation: $\bar{e}$
   c. twelve   f. vowel: e; pronunciation: $\bar{a}$
3. Ra—the tone on the descending scale that comes after Re. Pronunciation: Rä (*An a is used instead of an e because Re already has an e.*)
4. It borrows all the diatonic scale tones and all the syllable names.
5. The chromatic scale has twelve intervals; the diatonic scales have seven.
   It has all half-step intervals, whereas the diatonic contains five whole- and two half-step intervals.
6. They are produced by using accidentals.
7. Being able to sing the chromatic scale will help us sing the half steps produced by the accidentals on the staff.
8. Ti, Mi, Sol, Do, Re, Fa, Do, La
9. (Any one.)
   A handicap or disadvantage does not need to get us down.
   Using our talents for God's work will produce the most useful products.
   We must love Christ more than any earthly thing.

Lesson 12

Chapter 3, pp. 29–37
Review

1. scale   2. diatonic   3. major diatonic

4. home tone   6. mood   8. chromatic
5. minor diatonic   7. chromatic scale
9. ▲ Do, ● Re, ◆ Mi, ◤ Fa, ● Sol, ■ La, ♥ Ti, ▲ Do
10. ■ La, ♥ Ti, ▲ Do, ● Re, ◆ Mi, ◤ Fa, ● Sol, ■ La
11. Do, Di, Re, Ri, Mi, Fa, Fi, Sol, Si, La, Li, Ti, Do
    Do, Ti, Te, La, Le, Sol, Se, Fa, Mi, Me, Re, Ra, Do
12. Home tone: Do; La; Do
    No. of intervals: seven; seven; twelve
    No. of half-step intervals: two, two, twelve
    The half-step intervals using numerals: 3–4, 7–8; 2–3, 5–6
    Moods: happiness, contentment; sad, majestic, terrible
13. b
14. *(Be sure the students know the clef signatures and can letter the three staffs.)*

Sliding Modulator

On the last page of each pupil's book, you will find a sliding modular. The modulator can assist you in teaching transposition—a concept students often find difficult to master.

To use the sliding modulator, cut down through the middle of the wide line to separate the scale from the staff. Now you can slide the scale so that Do is on the fourth or fifth tone to illustrate transposition by fourths or fifths. The students can easily compare the intervals of the staff with the intervals of the scale to see where a sharp or flat is needed to make the intervals match.

To illustrate the second transposition, make temporary marks on the staff to show the changes made by the first transposition, and then slide the scale to the new key.

Lesson 13
Chapter 4, pp. 41–43
What Is a Key? What Is a Key Signature? What Is Transposition?

1. a. key   c. key tone
   b. key signature   d. transposition
2. scale; key
   The key has a fixed position on the staff and we know the absolute
     pitch of each note.
3. Home tone; Key tone
   Moveable; Fixed
   Three; Thirteen

4.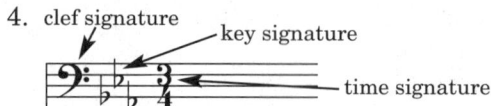
   clef signature
   key signature
   time signature

5. sharps
6. flats
7. It has no sharps or flats. *(The half steps of the scale exactly match the half steps of the staff.)*

Lesson 14

Chapter 4, pp. 43–48
Transposition by Fifths; Transposition by Fourths

1.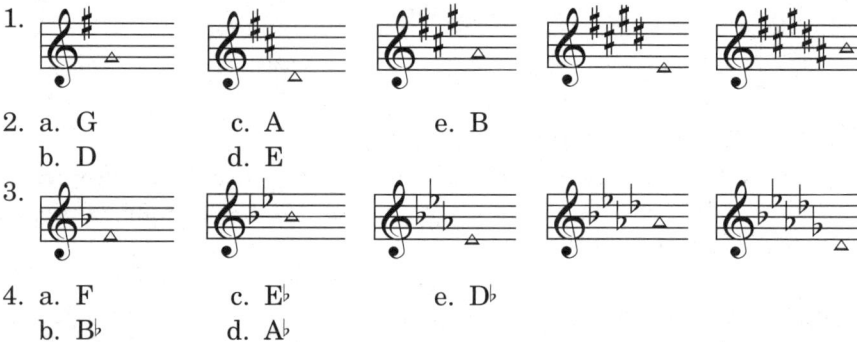

2. a. G   c. A   e. B
   b. D   d. E

3.

4. a. F   c. E♭   e. D♭
   b. B♭   d. A♭

5. To make the half steps of the staff line up with the half steps in the scale.

Lesson 15

Chapter 4, pp. 49–54
Transposition and Key Signatures; John Newton

1. G, D, A, E, B, F♯
   F, B♭, E♭, A♭, D♭, G♭

2.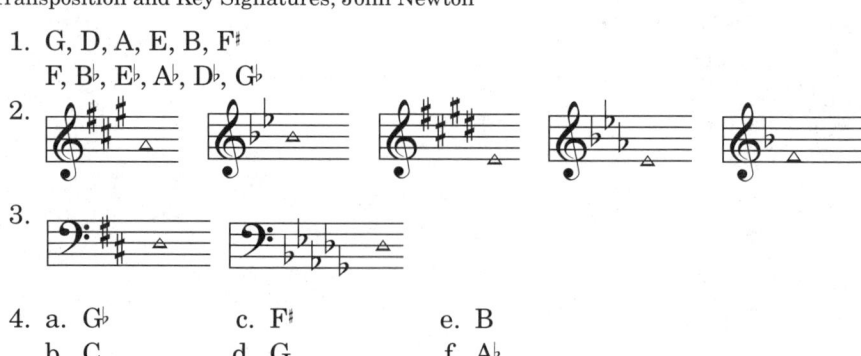

3.

4. a. G♭   c. F♯   e. B
   b. C   d. G   f. A♭
5. F
6. F♯

7. He read a book about Christ. Then a fierce storm nearly sank his ship. These experiences caused John to think seriously about Christ.

Extra

8. Sharps: F, C, G, D, A, E; Flats: B, E, A, D, G, C

Lesson 16
Chapter 4, pp. 41–53
Review

1. key
2. key tone
3. key signature
4. natural
5. transposing
6. transposition by fifths
7. sharps
8. transposition by fourths
9. flats
10. c
11. b

12.

13. a. G, D, A, E, B, F♯   b. F, B♭, E♭, A♭, D♭, G♭
14. a. B♭   b. E♭   c. D   d. A

Lesson 17
Chapter 5, pp. 57–61
Note and Rest Values; Characters That Affect Note Values

Note: Suggested songs numbers are given in brackets. All song numbers given are from the *Church Hymnal* unless otherwise indicated.

1. half
2. twice
3. a. ½   e. 1   h. 1
   b. ⅛   f. ¼   i. ⅛
   c. ¼   g. ¹⁄₁₆   j. ½
   d. ¹⁄₁₆

4. a. Hold (fermata)—indicates that a note or rest should be prolonged until the leader cuts it off. It usually doubles the value of the note or rest. [52, 143, 145, 370]
   b. Staccato mark—indicates that the note should be sung in a short, choppy manner; the note receives only one-fourth of its normal value. [185, 353, 431, 568]

   c. Semistaccato mark—indicates less accent than a staccato; the note should receive one-half of its normal value.

   d. Dot—increases the time value of the note to one-half again as much as the original value. A second dot increases the value one-half again as much as the first dot. [Dotted rest: 449—Alto in the chorus]

   e. Slur—placed under three or more notes of different pitch that are to be sung to the same word. [2, 93, 573]

   f. Triplet—three notes sung in the time of two notes of the same kind. Divides a beat in thirds instead of in half. [373]

   g. Tie—placed under two notes of the same pitch which are to be sung to one syllable. This makes possible a large number of note values. [546]

5. a. 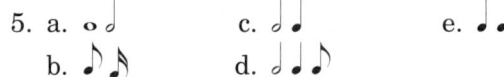   c.   e.

   b.   d.

Lesson 18

Chapter 5, pp. 61–63
Repeat Signs

1. a. D. C. al Fine [133, 411]

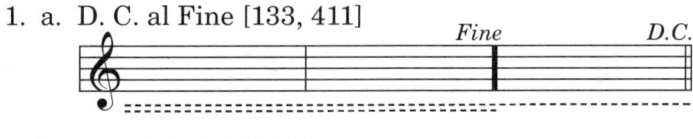

   b. repeat dots [61, 100]

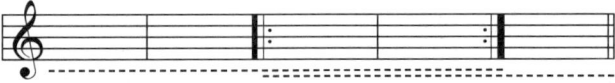

   c. D. S. al Fine [276, 259]

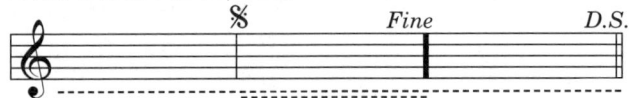

   d. repeat dots with first and second endings [20, 281]

2. Repeats can be used when the ending of a song uses music that is found earlier in the composition.

3. Repeats may also be used to give added emphasis. [*Christian Hymnal* #296, 656]

4. a. Da capo—repeat from the head, or beginning.

   b. Dal segno—return to the sign and repeat from there.

5. end
6. It marks the point from which music is to be repeated.

Lesson 19
Chapter 5, pp. 63–65
Pulse—Unit of Measure; What is a Measure?

1. a. pulse note   c. measure
   b. pulse   d. measure bar
2. The pulse note determines the length of the other notes. It also determines the beating pattern.
3. a. 4   c. ½   e. ¼
   b. 1   d. 3   f. 1
4. a. 2   c. ¼   e. 1½
   b. ½   d. 1

5.

6.

7. ♪ ♩ ♩

Lesson 20
Chapter 5, pp. 65–68
The Time Signature

1. a. time signature   b. primitive   c. derivative
2. He needs to know how many pulses are in a measure, and which note is the pulse note.
3. He can tell by looking at the time signature.
4. The song has three pulses in a measure.
   The half note is the pulse note.
5. a. ♩ 3   b. ♪ 6   c. ♪ 12
6. a.

   b.

7. (Individual work.)

Lesson 21
Chapter 5, pp. 68–69
Checking the Measure

1. smallest
2. a. ♩·   c. *o*   e. *o*
   b. *o·*   d. *o*   f. ♩·
3.
4.

Review

5. ♪
6. a. Hold (fermata)—indicates that a note or rest should be prolonged until the leader cuts it off. It usually doubles the value of the note or rest.
   b. Staccato mark—indicates that the note should be sung in a short, choppy manner; the note receives only one-fourth of its normal value.
   c. Semistaccato mark—indicates less accent than a staccato; the note should receive one-half of its normal value.
7. The song has two pulses in a measure.
   The quarter note is the pulse note.
8. a. 2   b. 2   c. 1   d. ½

Lesson 22
Chapter 5, pp. 69–74
Beating Patterns; Accent

1. a. compound   b. simple   c. beat
2. Beating time gives singing a sense of rhythm.
   It helps keep the leader on time.
   It helps keep the group together.
3. measure bar
4. Two-Beat   Three-beat   Four-beat

5. a. (Answer was given.)   d. simple, three-beat
   b. simple, two-beat   e. compound, four-beat
   c. compound, two-beat   f. compound, two-beat

6.

Lesson 23
Chapter 5, pp. 70–75
Accent; Charles Wesley

1. a. accent   b. primary accent   c. secondary accent
2. The first pulse after a measure bar is the strongest. (*There is only one primary accent in each measure.*)
3. the down beat
4. a. b. c. d.

5. a.

Bless-ed Bi-ble, how I love it! How it doth my bos - om cheer!

b.

And now, my soul, an - oth - er year Of thy short life is past;

c.

Now, gra-cious Lord, thine arm re - veal, And make thy glo - ry known;

6. Jesus, Lover of My Soul

Lesson 24
Chapter 5, pp. 57–74
Review

1. c
2. b
3. c

4. The song has three pulses in each measure.
The quarter note is the pulse note.

5. one
three

6. a. ♩   b. ♩ ▬   c. ♪ ૪   d. ○ ▬

7. a. ♫   b. ⌒   c. ⌒   d. ❘

    a. In a triplet, three notes are sung in the time of two notes of the same kind. It divides a beat in thirds instead of in half.

    b. A slur is placed under three or more notes of different pitch that are to be sung to the same word.

    c. A hold indicates that a note or rest should be prolonged until the leader cuts it off. It usually doubles the value of the note or rest.

    d. A staccato mark indicates that the note should be sung in a short, choppy manner; the note receives only one-fourth of its normal value.

8. a. ♩.   b. ♩.   c. ♪.   d. ♩.

9.

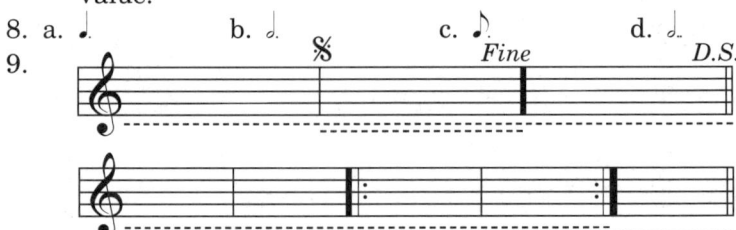

10. a. compound, three-beat   b. simple, two-beat

11. a. ♩.   b. ○

Lesson 25

Chapter 6, pp. 77–79
Observing the Mood and Message; Tempo

1. speed, volume, and style
2. (Any two.) Singing is not meaningful to them. They are not stirred by the message of song. The terms are not understood or are ignored.
3. tempo
4. a. andante [111, 183, 227]
    b. adagio [510]
    c. ritardando [275, 290, 543, 613]
    d. a tempo [275]
    e. presto
    f. moderato [480]
    g. accelerando
    h. allegro [505]

5. directions for singing slower

   In some communities there is a tendency to sing too fast.
6. accelerate; retard

Lesson 26

Chapter 6, pp. 79–83
Volume; Style; Isaac Watts

1. a. f—loudly [431, 510]
   b. mp—half soft (remember by *m*edium soft) [431]
   c. < >—gradually louder, then gradually softer [270, 510, 540, 594]
   d. p—softly [207, 440]
   e. ff—very loud
   f. pp—very soft [613]
   g. m—half voice (remember by *m*edium) [167, 510]
   h. mf—half loud (remember by *m*edium loud) [270]
2. a. cresc., <—gradually louder [207, 403, 448, 554]
   b. dim., >—gradually softer [167, 403, 448]
   c. decresc., >—gradually softer
3. from the words of the song
4. Good singing is medium in volume with room for variations to loud-
   ness and softness.
5. a. ♩ ♩ ♩   b. ♩ ♩ ♩   c. ♩ ♩ ♩   d. ♩ ♩ ♩
   a. Sing in a short, choppy manner; each note should receive one-
      fourth of their actual time value, with brief periods of rest
      between them.
   b. This is a milder form of staccato; each note should receive one-
      half of their actual time value, with brief periods of rest between
      them.
   c. Sing in a smooth, gentle style.
   d. Sing in a strongly accented style.
6. The singer must sense the message or general feeling of the words.
7. "When I Survey the Wondrous Cross"

Lesson 27

Chapters 1–5
Book Review

1. a. melodics   e. octave   i. measure bar
   b. trachea   f. chromatic   j. accidentals
   c. ledger lines   g. compound   k. natural
   d. larynx   h. rhythmics   l. diatonic

2. Middle C   brace   F clef   G clef   C clef

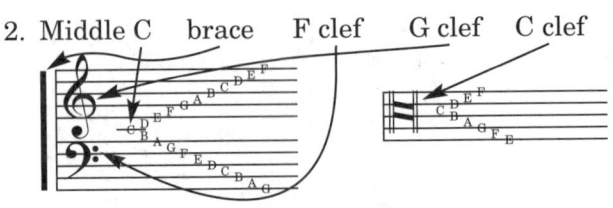

3. a. G♭   c. F♯   e. B
   b. C   d. G   f. A♭

4. a. double sharp   c. sharp
   b. double flat   d. flat

Lesson 28

Chapters 1–5
Book Review (continued)

1.

   a.   b.   c.   d.   e.   f.

2.   a.   b.   c.   d.   e.   f.

3. Major: happiness, contentment; Minor: sad, majestic, terrible

4. Di, Ri, Fi, Si, Li   Te, Le, Se, Me, Ra

5.

6. a. ♩ ♩   b. ♪ ♪   c. ♩ ♪ ♪

7. a. 1   b. 3   c. ½   d. 4

8. The song has six pulses in a measure.
   The eighth note is the pulse note.

9.

10.

    D   R   U   DR   U   D   R   U   DRU

Chapter One Test

1. a. vocal cords   d. power   f. voice culture
   b. larynx   e. trachea   g. cartilage
   c. rhythm
2. a. melodics; ~~tempo~~   b. rhythmics; ~~key~~   c. dynamics; ~~staff~~
3. Singing is most valuable when we understand and learn from the message.
4. (Any two.)
   Avoid very loud singing or speaking, especially if it becomes painful.
   Do not continually practice going to extreme ends of the scale, especially boys trying to sing bass.
   Do not force a husky voice; instead, relax it.
   If the voice is affected by a cold, do not force it or overuse it.
5. When air passes through tightened bands, called vocal cords, they vibrate, making a sound. *(The more air there is, the louder the sound is. The tighter the vocal cords are, the higher the pitch is.)*

Extra

6.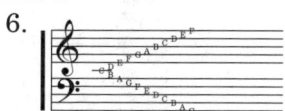

7. a. A♭   e. A   h. F♯   k. E
   b. G   f. E♭   i. D♭   l. D
   c. B   g. F   j. G♭   m. C
   d. B♭

Chapter Two Test

1. Middle C   brace   ledger line   F clef   G clef   C clef

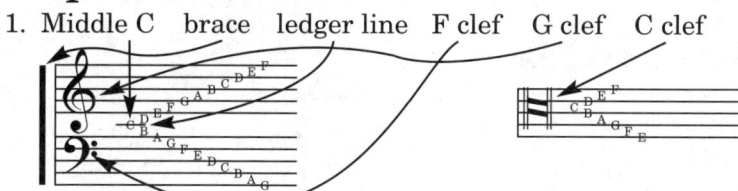

2. a. clef signature   c. accidentals   e. interval
   b. steps   d. degrees   f. grand staff
3. It is used in place of the G clef in songs for men's voices.
4. E–F; B–C
5. a. flat   c. double sharp   e. double flat
   b. natural   d. sharp

Chapter Three Test

1. La, Ti, Do, Re, Mi, Fa, Sol, La; Minor Diatonic Scale
2. Do, Re, Ti, Fa, Sol, La, Mi, Do; Major Diatonic Scale
3. Di, Ri, Mi, Fi, Sol, Si, Li, Ti
   Ti, Te, Le, Sol, Se, Fa, Me, Ra
4. a. home tone   c. diatonic   e. $\bar{e}$
   b. scale   d. octave   f. $\bar{a}$
5. sad, majestic, terrible
6. happiness, contentment
7.

	MAJOR SCALE	MINOR SCALE
Home Tone	Do	La
Syllable names of half-step intervals	Mi–Fa; Ti–Do	Mi–Fa; Ti–Do
Numbers of the notes with half-step intervals	3–4; 7–8	2–3; 5–6

Extra

8. a. Li   b. Di   c. Me   d. Ra
9.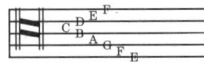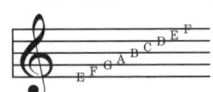

Chapter Four Test

1. a. key tone   e. sharps
   b. key signature   f. key
   c. scale   g. transposition by fourths
   d. transportation   h. flats
2. a. clef signature   b. key signature   c. time signature
3. a. G, D, A, E, B, F♯   b. F, B♭, E♭, A♭, D♭, G♭
4. They are needed to make the half steps of the scale match with the half steps of the staff.
5. a. D    b. B♭

6.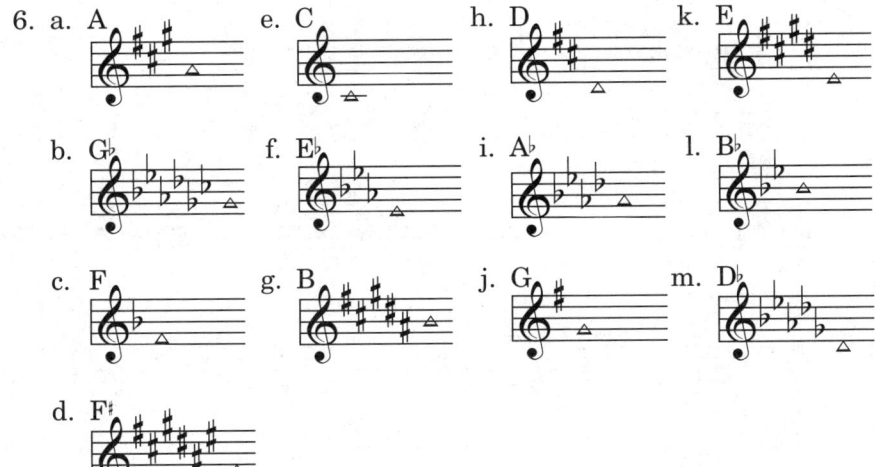

Chapter Five Test

1. a. ½   c. ¼   e. ¼
 b. ⅛   d. ¹⁄₁₆

2. a. slur b. triplet c. hold d. staccato mark

3.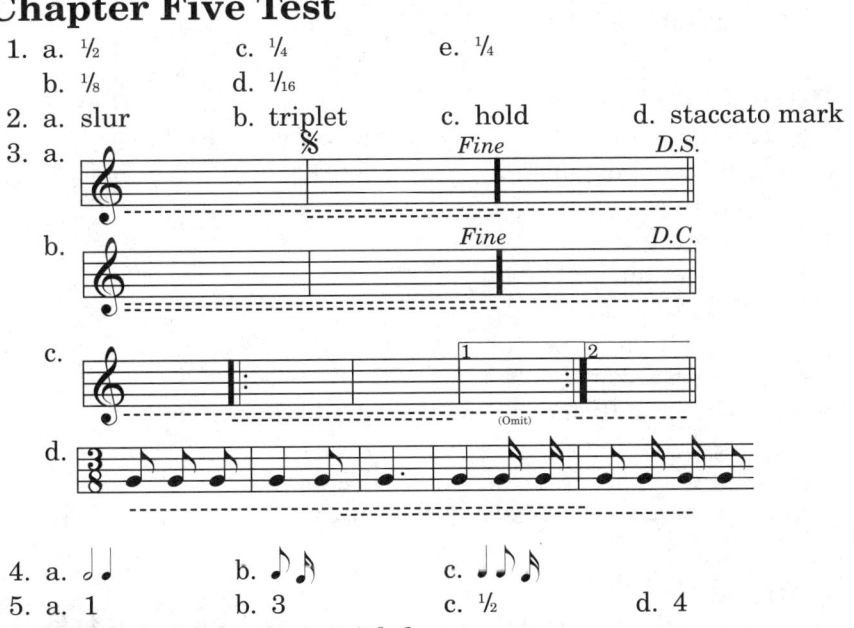

4. a.   b.   c.

5. a. 1 b. 3 c. ½ d. 4

6. half note, quarter note, eighth note

7. The song has six pulses in a measure.
   The eighth note is the pulse note.

8. a.

b.

9.

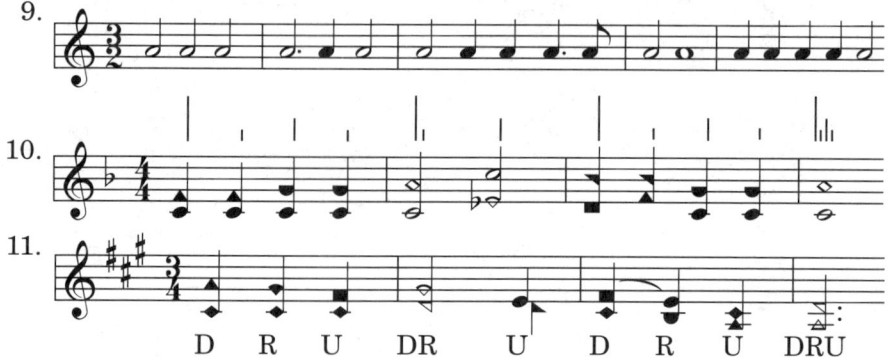

10.

11.

D   R   U   DR   U   D   R   U   DRU

12. a. simple, two-beat   c. simple, three-beat
    b. compound, two-beat   d. simple, four-beat

Chapter Six Test

1. a. ritardando c. a tempo   e. andante   g. moderato
   b. adagio   d. allegro   f. accelerando
2. a. f—loudly
   b. ff—very loudly
   c. m—medium; half voice
   d. mf—half loud
   e. mp—half soft
   f. pp—very soft
   g. < >—gradually louder and then gradually softer
   h. p—softly
3. a. dim., >   b. cres., <   c. decres., >
4. He gets clues from the words of the song.

Final Test

1.
   a. G♭   b. E   c. F♯   d. D♭   e. B
2. a. G–clef   b. F–clef   c. C–clef
3. a. natural—c   c. flat—e   e. double sharp—d
   b. double flat—b   d. sharp—a

4.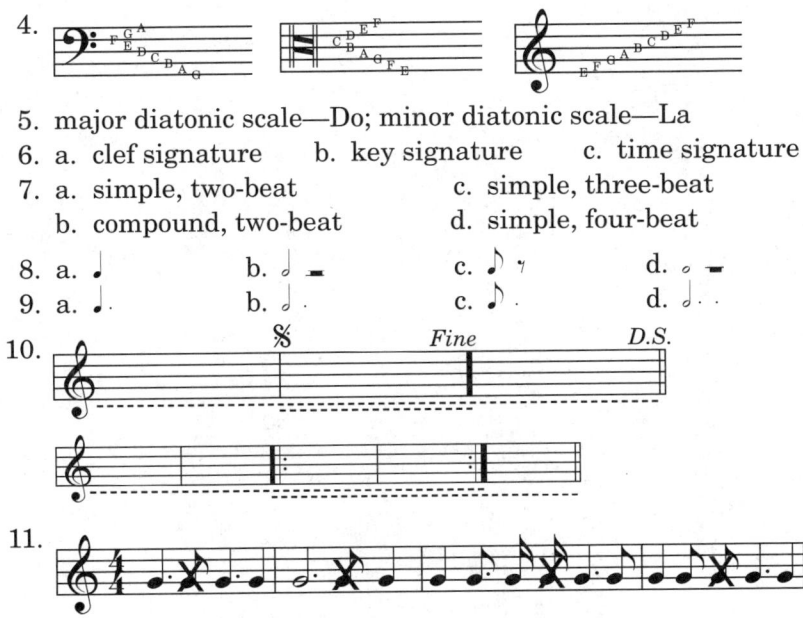

5. major diatonic scale—Do; minor diatonic scale—La
6. a. clef signature　　b. key signature　　c. time signature
7. a. simple, two-beat　　　　c. simple, three-beat
   b. compound, two-beat　　d. simple, four-beat
8. a. ♩　　b. ♩ ▬　　c. ♪ ⁊　　d. ○ ▬
9. a. ♩.　　b. ♩.　　c. ♪.　　d. ♩..

10.

11.

12. a. 2　　b. 2　　c. 1　　d. ½